UNCLE BILLY'S DOWNEAST BARBEQUE BOOK

Adventures in Barbeque

by Jonathan St. Laurent
& Charles Neave

Dancing Bear Books
West Rockport, Maine

Uncle Billy's Downeast Barbeque Book
Adventures in Barbeque
By Jonathan St. Laurent and Charles Neave

ISBN: 0-9622518-0-1

Dancing Bear Books
P.O. Box 4, Mt. Pleasant Street
West Rockport, Maine 04865
(207)236-6262

Library of Congress Cataloging-in-Publication Data

St. Laurent, Jonathan, 1950-
    Uncle Billy's Downeast Barbeque Book : adventures in barbeque
    by Jonathan St. Laurent, Charles Neave.
        p. cm.

    ISBN 0-9622518-0-1 :
    1. Barbeque cookery. 2. Uncle Billy's SouthSide Barbeque (Restaurant)
    I. Neave, Charles, 1953-   . II. Title.
    TX840.B3S7   1991   91-70126
    641.5'784—dc20   CIP

FIRST EDITION
Printed in the United States of America
10 9 8 7 6 5 4 3 2 1

Dancing Bear Books are distributed to the book trade by
Tilbury House, Publishers
The Boston Building, 132 Water Street, Gardiner, Maine 04345
(207)582-1899

Book and cover design by Tim Seymour, Timid Moon Designs.
Linoleum cuts by Kimber Lee Clark. Illustrations by Steven Priestley
and unknown napkin artist/patrons. Napkin template by Rod McCormick.
Editorial services by Caron Leichtman. Photography by Phil Rogers.

Acknowledgments

The authors thank a number of people for their help along the way: Karen Curtin for her heroic mural; Steve Priestley for the instant excellence and fine art adorning the walls, menus and such at Uncle Billy's; Phil Rogers for always having the camera ready and the spirit willing: Rod McCormick for the right napkin at the right time; John Cardano for sharing schemes; Stewart Blackburn, of Stache Foods, fine chef and friend; the cast and crew of Uncle Billy's, who kept the joint afloat and smoking while others were off writing a book; Marge and Eddie Griffin, Jonny's effervescent landlords who gave "the kid" a chance; The Madame and the Boys for the time away from them; Rosie and the girls for the space; Jonathan's father Alec for his encouragement, and for his help with the plumbing and electrical; Attorney Henry Berry III and his wife Susan for their generous help and humor; Tom Rousell and Jim Ledue, of Alberta's Restaurant, Portland; The good doctor, J.P. and Mary Herzog for sharing the vision; Missy Chapman, Park Morrison, Maureen Egan and Trisha Johanson for reading; Kerry for painstakingly making this book happen; Ranger Mel somewhere deep in Texas; John Willingham for setting the example; and, of course, Uncle Billy for the inspiration. May they all end up in Barbeque Heaven.

Also, thanks to Ronnie.

Napkin art no. 9

This Book is Dedicated
to the Memory of
ALICE O'DONNELL

Uncle Billy's Mother and Nephew Jonny's Grandmother

☘

"She taught my mother to cook, who then taught me to cook."
— Jonathan A. St. Laurent

Contents

Foreword

A friend of mine kept on about Uncle Billy's. His enthusiasm for this barbeque joint in South Portland permeated every conversation. He was either calling from Uncle Billy's, or was just leaving for lunch at Uncle Billy's, or was leaving Uncle Billy's things behind at my house, like Death By Chocolate sauce, then Voodoo Jerk Slather — "It's for chicken," he said as he left that afternoon. I've never forgiven him for not warning me about the rubber gloves.

During my next trip to Portland I went to Uncle Billy's and met Jonathan St. Laurent. Jonathan was in a transitional phase, somewhere between the fine chef and dessert creator he had been when my palate first became acquainted with his considerable talents, and Nephew Jonny, the barbeque champion of Maine and Uncle Billy's favorite relative.

Uncle Billy is a real guy; a man with a happy spirit and a ready smile. The restaurant that bears his name and trumpets his spirit, however, is all Jonathan's doing. Uncle Billy's preference for barbeque thrills his nephew's culinary skills. Uncle Billy and Nephew Jonny are, to put it quite mildly, unique individuals, characters of a different spice.

Which is how it should be. Barbeque is not about

being unassuming. It's food you wipe from the corner of your mouth with a backhand swipe of your index finger. Barbeque is flavor of life as much as it is flavor of food. It is an adventure your palate takes your mind on. The walls at Uncle Billy's SouthSide Barbeque, which is the name of Jonathan's restaurant, attest to this. The memorabilia hanging from them, sometimes precariously, ranges from a 40-year old photo of Billy in his baseball playing days, to patrons' renditions of pork heaven inked onto barbeque sauce stained napkins and plaster of Paris pork snouts.

As you travel through this book, you'll meet the people with whom Uncle Billy likes to keep company. They are the people of Uncle Billy's life as told in barbeque. There was a time I thought Ranger Mel, Judge D.T. Childs, the vegetarian who works in the smokehouse with Jonny at Uncle Billy's SouthSide Barbeque, were all made up. I didn't question the stories, not for a second, that Jonathan was telling me as I ate my first Uncle Billy's lunch — a pork shoulder sandwich, side of Billy Beans, Mother's Mountain Coleslaw and a few pints of Geary's ale, all followed by a Death By Chocolate Sundae — they were so obviously made up. But then Jonathan said something about the portable cooker trailer rig out back that Ranger Mel helped him build.

"Hold on," I said, "What do you mean he helped you?"

Jonathan went on to explain how everyone's idea of the best way to cook and eat barbeque varies by at least twice the number of people cooking it. You don't just make barbeque, you live barbeque. Cookers, cooking techniques and instruments, native spices and local flavors are the conversation of barbeque chefs, cooks and showmen. Barbeque is more than a cuisine, it's an experience.

"Wait a minute, hold on, Ranger Mel is a person?"

Jonathan looked at me, his expression saying of course he's a person, what the hell did you think he was — a rock band?

The previous hour was filled with stories about big, burly guys buying pounds of barbequed brisket to snack on as they drove to their plywood home deep in the woods somewhere west of Portland, stories of a small Vietnamese woman who makes a great pork sandwich and keeps a bottle of brandy under the counter for her favorite customers, Uncle Billy to name one, and then the story about the stag party and kerosene heater and the hundred-dollar bills that I eventually edited out of the book — these stories, like Ranger Mel, were all true?

"Well, yes, mostly completely true. Sometimes it gets kinda blurry."

Amongst the stories, reminiscences and lies there are, as Uncle Billy would no doubt say, some damn fine recipes here. You don't need a lot of cooking experience or special equipment; the ability to read English and a coverable grill will do in most cases. The pages up front explain cookers and fires and, in general, encourage you not to be scared off by how good barbeque tastes, anyone can cook it. We've also tried to bring a little Uncle Billy into your life. And we're not the least bit sorry about it.

Kerry Leichtman
Publisher
Dancing Bear Books

Introduction to
Downeast Barbeque, America's Original Barbeque

Downeast barbeque. The phrase reads like a contradiction. While it might seem a bit strange, especially to our friends in Texas and Tennessee and Kansas City and such, that a born and bred Yankee of French-Canadian descent and classical French culinary training is messing about with *their* barbeque. We kindly, respectfully and most gently, point out that America's first barbeque took place right here in Downeast Maine. What is a clam bake if not clam barbeque? Jonny's Acadian ancestors were steaming clams and lobster, and roasting venison with the native Indian population while the forbears of the westward pioneers were still Europeans trying to scrape up passage to the New World.

We'd be the last to start an argument over this, and in fact are quite respectful of the way barbeque has developed at the pits, pig palaces and rib joints across the United States' southern tier. While, for whatever their reason, New England cooks were putting everything that walked, crawled, flew and swam into baking crocks or boiling water, the populace of the southern and westward territories cooked, and continued to develop, barbeque. Our hats of appreciation are off to them.

Jonny learned his trade apprenticing throughout the kitchens of Europe and eating his way, sometimes with

Uncle Billy, across the American South. This traveling road show of theirs brings all manner of influences into Uncle Billy barbeque cookery. What makes Downeast barbeque special is this melting pot approach to cooking, where flavors are created from memories, intuition and necktie stains.

Inspiration and ingredients for Uncle Billy Barbeque originated with people and places all over the world. Combine a Caribbean-inspired jerk sauce with Maine lobster and you begin to see seafood in a new light. Actually, if you put Jonny's Voodoo Jerk Slather Sauce on just about anything it will glow, providing a new light of its own.

The spirit of barbeque is the same no matter where it's cooked, or who cooked it first. In some circles a chef's bravado is almost as important as his pork shoulder, unless, of course, it's just empty boasting. As Uncle Billy says, "If he can't make a good pork shoulder sandwich he had better keep his loud mouth shut."

If you're already familiar with barbeque cooking, jump right on ahead to the recipes. If barbeque is a new experience for you, stay here with us for just a few minutes and we'll take you through the basics.

An important thing to realize right away is that the typical barbeque chef doesn't look like a rocket scientist for a good reason — he usually isn't. Barbeque is simple, especially when someone else has developed the recipes. It is a technique of roasting food using fire and smoke. The trick to cooking barbeque is learning to control how much heat and smoke your fire creates. Aside from that, if you've ever roasted a marshmallow on a stick you've already got the idea.

It's hard to go wrong cooking barbeque as long as you cook it low and slow. Words — in the minds of barbequers everywhere — to live, and cook, by.

As you'll discover, the cuts of meat used in real barbeque don't vary much, nor do they cost much. Barbeque is a good, honest, working-people style of cooking that came about through necessity. Poor people and slaves didn't have kitchens and cooking equipment, only a fire for cooking.

Uncle Billy's nephew Jonny works in a smokehouse he built out behind the restaurant. It can hold two whole hogs; or a few big turkeys, 20 feet of link sausage, close to 100 chickens and probably 50 pounds of brisket. Your needs, however, are easily met with just about any kind of store-bought or homemade grill that has a cover and allows you to control the air draft. Cookers are explained, as much as they need be, just ahead in Tools, Fuels and Rules.

Cooking with heat and smoke, rather than just cooking over an open fire, is the difference between making barbeque and grilling food. Just sprinkle a handful of soaked and chipped wood on your charcoal briquets or lava rocks, close the lid and you've made the transition from grilling to barbequing. Fruitwood, mesquite and other smoking woods have become easier to get over the last year or so. Many supermarkets and most specialty foods stores sell chipped woods for barbeque, as do many mail order catalogs. Kingsford, the charcoal briquet people, produce a nice mesquite-laced briquet. We'll get into some of the details in the next chapter.

Although none of the recipes are hard, you'll find a good mix, from the dead simple to those with a million ingredients and a page or so of instructions. Go with your mood. Feel like spending most of a beautiful Sunday sitting out back with a cooler of brews and a pair of speakers between your ears? Then go ahead and cook a brisket. If you don't want to make a day of it Pork Tenders will do you fine. Make an adventure out of a rainy day by mixing a big batch of barbeque sauce. There's plenty to chose from.

Barbeque sauce recipes typically come with yard-

long ingredient lists. No barbeque book should be with
out a good sauce recipe (and Jonny doesn't give out his
without wondering what the hell's the matter with him),
but you shouldn't *have* to make your own sauce. We'll
say it right up front: It's perfectly acceptable to use store-
bought barbeque sauce. If making your own seems like
too much work yet pouring from the jar seems like not
enough, Jonny's developed a recipe for enhancing the
barbeque sauce that you buy at the supermarket.

In the back of the book is a glossary, just to make
sure we're communicating. Also in the back is a resource guide you can use to send away for the stuff you
can't find at your corner grocer.

Barbeque is fun; fun to cook, fun to eat, and fun to
think about cooking and eating. Go ahead, dig right in
and tell them Uncle Billy sent you.

Some Log Rolling
on Spirits of the Hop, Grape and Potato

We thought it best to offer some guidance on the use
and imbibement of alcoholic beverages as they pertain to
barbeque.

We hope you'll notice that despite the gallons of
various and sundry alcohol-based beverages consumed
throughout these barbeque adventures, no one ever

gets behind the wheel of a car, yoke of an airplane (or snowmobile), or tries to operate heavy machinery during said intake. It is not coincidence that Uncle Billy's preferred mode of travel (since they stopped running passenger trains through Portland) is Greyhound Bus.

A barbeque without alcohol is like a pig without ribs. To John Willingham, America's foremost barbeque pitmaster, a barbeque is a social event; a party, a gathering of people having a good time, where the beer can be as much a centerpiece as the food. A sentiment wholeheartedly ascribed to by Uncle Billy and Nephew Jonny.

Here in New England we're enjoying a resurgence of the local micro-brewery and brew pub. The fresh beers and ales they produce are tremendous. The tap at Uncle Billy's features Portland-brewed Geary's Ale. We can't think of a barbeque dish it doesn't complement.

Should wine be your preference, we've suggested varietals, but they are merely suggestions. Uncork, or unscrew, whatever pleases your palate. And that includes iced tea and soda pop. As long as you enjoy it, it's barbeque.

bar•be•que (bär′ be kyōō′) *

/Fr.Amer./N.Eng./S.Portld., Me./Jonny StL./
1. To roast food using an open fire and smoke. 2.
A technique of cooking that dates back to cave-
men using meat flavored with fire smoke and,
more recently, hot spices. 3. A social event at
which meat is cooked, liquid refreshment is liberally consumed and a good time is had by all.
(also) Anglo.Amer/ barbecue, BBQ, Bar-B-Que

* Consider all those rib joints with twisted neon letters flashing BBQ
and B-B-Q and Bar-B-Que overhead. Not likely there are many that say
Bar-B-Cue. Now imagine you own a barbeque restaurant and you
don't want to write out "barbecue" every time you have to write the
name of the restaurant on a return address or check or something.
What would you do, abbreviate it to BBC? If you did, people would
expect Masterpiece Theater, not a plate of ribs. So Webster be
damned, we're spelling it our way. Uncle Billy says his Nephew Jonny
is just a lousy speller.

TOOLS, FUELS & RULES

Cooking Rigs
·
Fuels and Flavors
·
Three Options for Building a Fire
·
Barbeque Tools

Everyone is different. Good thing, otherwise there wouldn't be so much neat barbeque stuff at the store.

The number of tools and such that you actually need is quite small. Still if you like collecting gadgets, barbeque is going to be your kind of recreation. Uncle Billy has been know to carry a zip-lock baggie full of hardwood chips when invited to a country club party. Gas grills, in the hands of the inexperienced, can be fairly bland eating. A few well tossed soaked-chips later, and there's barbeque cooking over the lava rocks.

Cooking Rigs

There are a lot of good barbeque rigs available to you. We've squeezed the selection into four cooker types (five if you include gas grills), all the right size for a backyard setup. Some pretty impressive party and commercial rigs are also available, should you consider getting into barbeque in a major league way. Each cooking rig has advantages inherent to its design.

Kettle cookers are versatile, can function as a simple grill, a slow-cook smoker and an oven. If imitation is truly the sincerest form of flattery, the Weber Company has been flattered beyond measure by many, many other manufacturers. Weber offers a variety of great kettle cookers. We use it as the standard against which other kettle cookers must measure up. A kettle grill is a sturdy-built barbeque with an efficient vent/draft design. With easily adjustable vents under the charcoal and over the food, cooking temperatures are easy to regulate. The bottom flue doubles as an ash sweeper, making clean-up an easy chore. When you have finished cooking, close both dampers to create an airtight seal that snuffs out the live coals. This not only eliminates the danger of leaving live coals on your back deck, it also preserves the coals for reuse next time you fire up the grill.

Kettle cookers are available in every department store, mall, and most hardware and outdoor supply stores across the U.S. and Canada. They come in a variety of sizes and colors, and with options like built-in thermometers (which are nice if you have the money). You can swing by the mall in the afternoon and pick up a Weber, using your trusty credit card, and be making barbeque that evening.

Custom-made barrel rigs are Uncle Billy's cooker of choice, probably because he doesn't like malls, doesn't have a credit card so couldn't go to a mall to buy a cooker anyway, and because you can fit more food on one. Jonny uses barrel cookers at home, at catering parties and just outside the restaurant's kitchen door to give foods one last shot of direct heat before serving. Barrel cookers also appeal to Billy and Jonny's thrifty Yankee nature. If you can weld, or have a friend who welds, a barrel cooker is downright cheap.

Get your friend to cut a 55-gallon metal barrel in half, lengthwise, while you go to the hardware store and the scrap metal yard to pick up the rest of what you'll need, which includes a couple of carriage bolts, some angle steel, expanded metal for the grill and a six-pack of beer. A good welder can work out most of what you'll need from the illustration, or you can send for detailed plans from the Acadian Smoke Wizards listed in the Where to Find Barbeque Stuff Resource Guide at the back of the book.

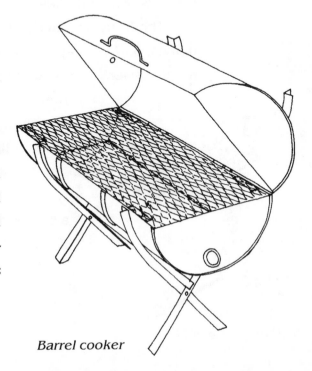

A couple of pointers, though. Avoid barrels that are stamped with a skull and crossbones icon, usually accompanied by words like, "Hazardous Waste." And be sure to burn off all the slag, barrel waste, paint and whatever else has adhered to the barrel, before using the thing to cook with.

Barrel cooker

For the well-heeled barbequer, **water/smoker cookers** are worth consideration. These cylindrical cookers are efficient to use and safe to operate. They allow you to control cooking temperatures with a great degree of accuracy.

Although narrow, water/smoker cookers hold a surprising amount of food. The typical rig has a bottom grill-shelf for charcoal, another grill-shelf to hold a water/drip pan, and two more grill-shelves above that for food. Some models even have a few hooks along the top rim for hanging poultry and ribs. The better models, like the Smoke N' Grill and the Cajun Cooker have extras like wooden handles and a temperature gauge.

These cookers, like kettle cookers, are getting easier to find in malls and catalogs. L.L. Bean carries a full line of Brinkman's cookers, which makes owning one as easy as dialing the telephone.

The fourth cooker is a handy piece of specialty equipment that makes barbequing over an open campfire, or in your fireplace, much easier. A **Tuscan brazier grill** is a vertically-adjustable grill

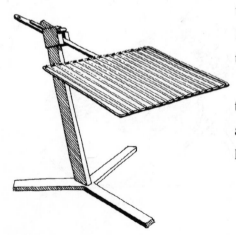

that holds food over an open fire. Not a common barbeque tool, make one yourself or order from the Acadian Smoke Wizards.

The **gas grill** is our least favorite cooker. The typical gas grill uses a propane-fueled fire to heat a bed of rocks. The problem is rocks don't smoke. If you're grill shopping, get something else. If you

Tuscan brazier grill

already have a gas grill, you'll have to do a bit more conjuring to work the sorcery of fire and smoke. Make sure you use plenty of soaked chips when cooking to create plenty of that good wood smoke (soaked rocks just fizzle a lot), and be sure to scrape the drippings off the rocks every once in a while.

Fuels and Flavors

Jonny mostly fuels Oprah, his eight-foot double-barrel stack cooker out behind the restaurant, in the parking lot next to Eddie Griffin's barroom, with red oak or maple logs burned down to smoldering coals. Backyard Webers, barrel cookers and water cookers are better suited to charcoal than split logs. The more you know about charcoal, the better. Fortunately, there's not much to know.

At home the best fuels you can use are **natural wood charcoals**. They're smoldered under controlled conditions producing a hot, long-lasting burn and a flavorful smoke. Some folks in Connecticut are making hardwood charcoal using the same basic technology as the Yaqui Indians, who are still making charcoal from mesquite in Mexico, as they have for generations. One advantage to natural wood charcoal is that you can start cooking as soon as the fire is lit. There's no waiting for the coals to catch or burn down, as with briquets. They also produce less ash. However, natural charcoal isn't always easy to find and can be messy to handle.

Fortunately, some good **charcoal briquets** are also available.

Kingsford's been at it for 50 years, having distributed Henry Ford's coal substitute invention when it was first introduced to the market. They also make a mesquite-laced briquet.

Briquets are only partially charcoal. They are also a varied mixture of ingredients that can include coal dust, sawdust, tar and petroleum-based adhesives. The difference between the good and not-so-good briquet is the recipe used to create them. The advantages to briquets are that they burn evenly, are reasonably priced, and are sold everywhere. When using any briquet, let it burn until the coals are coated with a thin layer of white ash, letting the nasty stuff burn off before you start to cook. Do not, under any circumstances, burn briquets indoors. A few of our recipes call for cooking in your fireplace at home. Use wood for those recipes.

Some recipes, the ones that require more than a couple hours of cooking time, have you stoke the fire by adding more coals. Natural charcoal can be put directly into the cooker, but if you're using briquets you'll have to burn them down to a thin layer of white ash before adding to a grill loaded with food. You might consider starting your fire with briquets and feeding it with natural charcoal as needed while cooking.

In either case, barbequing is more than cooking with heat, it's cooking with heat and smoke. The sorcery is in the smoke. You'll get some smoke using charcoal, but charcoal needs to be supplemented with **wood chips** soaked in something — mostly water, but sometimes whiskey or wine is nice. When soaked wood or corn cob chips are tossed onto a charcoal fire, it creates a flavorful smoke that permeates the food.

We use handfuls as a measurement in the recipes. The rule of thumb is to toss on a handful of chips when you begin to cook, a second handful after two hours if the recipe calls for a cooking time longer than two hours, and a third handful after four hours for a six-hour cook. The recipes will guide you.

The most commonly used **hardwood chips** are hickory, mesquite, white and red oak. They burn long and smoky, and have strong distinctive flavors. They are better with beef than with fish and poultry. **Fruitwood chips**, like apple, cherry and plum are lighter and sweeter, like their fruits, and are used more with poultry and fish.

Alder is good with almost everything. Despite its abundance here in Maine, nobody wants to harvest it. Uncle Billy and Jonny cut down bunches at Billy's place and pile it in the back of Melvin, Jonny's pickup. They bring it to the Cape Elizabeth dump, along with a pork sandwich drenched in Killer Gene's Tar Heel Vinegar Sauce for the fellow who operates the town chipper. One load is enough for a year. In a pinch, Jonny planes off alder shavings, or any wood for that matter, using his Makita planer, though Uncle Billy always gives him hell for not buying American.

TIPS ON CHIPS

When using chips, soak them for at least two hours before cooking. If you're endowed with the ability to plan ahead, soak them the night before. To soak, put the chips in a bowl and pour in enough liquid to cover the chips. When your fire is ready for the food, toss on the soaked chips, just before the food.

Chipped corn cobs make delicious smoke, but are tricky to find. Your best bet is to buy some from a local smokehouse. Don't get carried away and cut off something important trying to plane a corn cob.

Juniper is abundant here in Maine. Harvest by cutting into six-inch lengths and toss them right on the fire. If they're dried out, soak them like chips. **Fir boughs, grape vines** and **lilac clippings** smoke well when freshly snipped. Try some when you're feeling adventurous. Watch out for the fir though, it's strong and flavorful, and also quite flammable, but delicious with fish.

Three Options for Building a Fire

The **chimney starter** is a clever tool, and our favorite for starting charcoal fires. All you do is crumple up some newspaper and put it in the bottom, cover with a little dry kindling, and top with charcoal. Light the newspaper with a match and in a few minutes the whole package will be burning. Using a handle, thick woodstove gloves or fireplace tongs, dump the coals out of the chimney starter into your

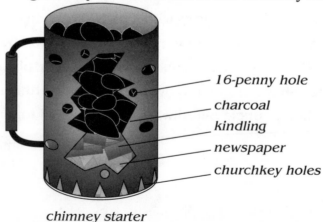

16-penny hole
charcoal
kindling
newspaper
churchkey holes

chimney starter

cooker and mix them with the rest of your charcoal. If using natural charcoal, the fire is ready for cooking. If you're using charcoal briquets, wait until the coals are covered with a thin layer of white ash before cooking, as we've said before.

Chimney starters can be purchased from cooking supply stores, by mail order, or you can make your own. We like the last choice because the materials are free, making this a thrifty Yankee's ideal tool. Use either a quart-size juice can, or better yet, go to a restaurant and ask for a #10-size can. Lots of what restaurants buy comes in #10 cans, and they're saving dumpster space by giving you one. These #10 cans are bigger than quart cans, which will let you start more charcoal at once.

Clean the can, pull off the paper label and, using a can opener, or church key (Uncle Billy calls them his "redneck powertool"), ring the bottom perimeter of the can with can-opener holes then punch or drill more holes around the side of the can, using the can opener, a 16-penny nail or quarter-inch drill bit. That's it, unless of course, you decide to rivet a handle to the thing. We recommend that you do, it will be a lot less tricky to handle.

Electric starters work very well. They don't start as many coals at once as the chimney starter, and they cost $15 to $20 — which is $15 to $20 more than a homemade chimney starter — and sometimes there's no plug at the campsite or party grounds. But when there is, they start fires quickly and without additives. If we didn't have a chimney starter we'd probably use one.

Starter fluid is easy to use and is a no-fuss way to get a load of charcoal briquets going. Just make sure the fluid has completely burned away before you put any food on the grill. No sense having your food taste like a West Texas oil field. Try to abstain from using starter fluid with natural charcoal, it defeats the purpose. Mesquite charcoal is so damn explosive already, you'd be foolish to make it any more ornery. Don't be wearing shorts when you light mesquite charcoal.

How much charcoal to use, depends on whether you use natural charcoal or briquets. With briquets, it depends on what brand you use, they're all different. What kind of food you're cooking, how much food, how long will it cook and at what temperature must also be considered. Natural charcoal burns hotter and longer than briquets so you'll need less. If you're cooking over a direct heat, start enough charcoal to make a single layer of coals directly under the food. With briquets make it a tight layer, with natural charcoal make it a loose layer. Figure charcoal quantities for indirect heat the same way. Even though you don't layer the coals directly underneath the food, determine how much charcoal to use by figuring it as if you were.

Direct heat

Indirect heat

A **direct heat** means the food is cooked directly over the live coals. An **indirect heat** means you should pile the coals somewhere other than under the food. This way the food receives heat but will not drip onto the coals, which causes flare-ups and scorching. When cooking over an indirect heat, which is the way most barbeque is cooked, the proximity of the food to the coals will, in part, determine cooking temperatures. When using an indirect heat source, pile the charcoals rather than layer them, freeing up more grill space overhead. Where you place the pile is up to you. Some people pile them off to one side, while others pile the coals in the middle and then circle the grill's surface with food.

Barbeque Tools

You've probably picked up on the fact that we're not into fancy gear. We like to use stuff that's already kicking around the house, or that you can pick up at a yard sale or the Five and Dime store. You can wear one of those aprons and hats with the funny sayings on it if you want, but wait until Uncle Billy's gone home before you do — he tends to accidentally spill things on them.

You really do need:

A pair of 18-inch stainless steel spring **tongs**.

A **spritzer**, like the kind you mist plants with. Fill with water, set it on stream spray and use it to control flare-ups.

A good strong **chef's fork**, the longer and sturdier the handle the better.

A nylon bristle **paintbrush** for basting and slathering stuff. Even better, and cheaper, use a cotton **string mop**.

Good heavy cloth **oven mitts** from a good kitchen supply house.

Heavy, industrial-weight **rubber gloves**, like oil deliverymen wear here in Maine when they yank the big hoses out of their fuel trucks.

Lightweight **rubber kitchen gloves** are useful when rubbing and slathering hot sauces like Voodoo Jerk Slather Sauce.

A small **meat thermometer.** The kind that registers quickly and clips to your pocket is best. Sometimes these are called gourmet meat thermometers. They'll dial up the temperature real quick so you don't have to keep the cover off the cooker too long.

When it comes to spending money on tools, don't skimp on the **fish grill.** Get the most heavy duty grill you can find. It should have strong clamps and hinges, and long handles. It's useful for camping trips and fireplace cooking if you don't have a Tuscan brazier grill.

A metal bread pan makes an ideal **drip pan,** so do steel pie plates when placed between the coals to catch drippings for gravies and gyppos.

Cooking Temperature Chart	Indirect	Direct
Low heat	200 to 275°F	450 to 650°F
Medium	325°F	650 to 850°F
Hot	Over 375°F	850 to 1000°F

Five-gallon galvanized **trash cans** are the safest way we know for ash disposal. After cooking, clean the ashes out of the cooker and into the ash can. Close the lid and leave them for at least a day before dumping, coals can smolder a long time.

You'll find a **fireplace shovel** useful for moving ashes from cooker to ash can to final dumping ground. Fireplace tools are prime yard sale pickings. A shovel will probably go for a buck, 50 cents if the people are trying to move a bunch of them.

Napkin art no. 007

Aside from that, stock up on plates, forks, knives, napkins, glasses, sunglasses (if it's nice out), and all the other **stuff** you're likely to need, want and be willing to die for. Knock yourself out.

"Now get on with it," as Uncle Billy would say.

PORK

Pork Shoulder Sandwich and the Story
of Uncle Billy's SouthSide Barbeque
·
Bastid Spare Ribs
·
Rib End Sandwiches
·
Pork Tenders
·
Bus Station Saigon Sandwiches
·
Backwoods Bourbon Whole-Log
Arkansas Round Steak

Sunday dinner at Grandmother Alice's meant roast pork, mashed potatoes with pork gravy and whatever vegetables were fresh. "Meat and two veg," is what the English call it. "Pahk dinnah" is what people in Maine call it.

Jonny spends more time with pork ribs and butts than with anything else. What makes pork such great eating? The answer lies in the wood and the smoke. It is the sorcery that takes place on the grill that transforms pork to barbeque. The bastes, sauces and rubs are important, but cooking with wood and smoke is what barbeque is really all about.

Finding quality pork is as simple as finding a good butcher, one who will cut meat to specification. The person behind the meat counter who takes pride in his work is your ally. Befriend and appreciate him and he will take care of you.

The availability of various cuts of pork can be a regional matter. The skin-on pork shoulders that are readily available to barbequers in the South is a Boston butt up North. Soul food staples like jowls and chitter-lings are readily available at supermarkets throughout the South, while in New England cured picnics for boiled dinners and salt pork for baked beans are more common. Work with your butcher to get the right cuts. If all else fails, don't give up, improvise.

The flavor of pork also varies, region to region. Folks in Georgia like their hogs peanut-fed; in New England we rely on Yankee know-how (garden and restaurant scraps). As a matter of fact, there's one fellow in Bowdoinham who feeds his hogs ground shark meat. When Jonny first laid eyes on one of those hogs he thought its sleek shape resembled a greyhound dog more than a pig. Turned out, the meat from those hogs was leaner than any pork Jonny had eaten before; a delicious, lean mean porcine cuisine — not a hint of shark flavor anywhere — not even in its fins.

To a lot of folks in Maine — and elsewhere — pork ribs are called spare ribs, although at Uncle Billy's they're called bastid ribs. These are as versatile as they are tasty and shouldn't be confused with what are called country spare ribs in New England and *Arkansas ribs* down South. These aren't real ribs; they're sawed-up pieces of bone with some meat hanging on. While they'll do in a pinch, especially if the market has them on special, realize the meat is closer to a pork chop than a pork rib. Uncle Billy won't eat them, but you're more than welcome to substitute them if that's your pleasure. Pork is pork after all, and pork cooked low and slow is barbeque.

Making bastid-cut spare ribs requires trimming, either by you or your butcher. Buy what's called a *three and down* rib, which means the rack (or slab) should weigh three pounds or less — should, but won't, they usually weigh closer to three and a half pounds. The collarbone and breast plate are trimmed away so that later your guests will be able to cut the ribs with a steak knife.

Jonny recommends trimming the racks yourself since the process is not that involved and after one or two tries you'll have it down pat. Just keep your cleaver sharp and your fingers out of the way. No matter who does the trimming, don't throw those trimmings away, be sure to cook them along with the ribs for making Rib End Sandwiches, or just serve them on their own, with barbeque sauce on the side, as Trash Ribs.

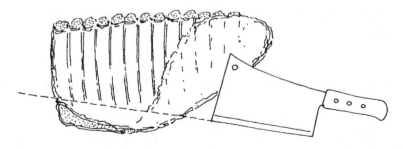

Pork Shoulder Sandwich and the Story of Uncle Billy's SouthSide Barbeque

For the purist, barbeque is pork shoulder — period. It's an understandable attitude, especially after you've tasted one. Pork used to be the only four-legged critter on the menu at Uncle Billy's. The shoulder portion is the essential barbeque cut of pork. Believe it or not, there's a sizable number of barbeque aficionados here in Maine — expatriated Texans, Kansans and Southerners, as well as a few born and bred New Englanders. Nephew Jonny can talk about beef brisket and jerk lobster to these folks until closing time, but he's never going to change a single purist's mind. That's fine with Jonny, he takes every pork shoulder sandwich they order as a compliment.

It was barbequed pork shoulder that got Uncle Billy and his nephew working together on developing barbeque recipes. Jonny began his career working and apprenticing as a chef in fancy restaurants the world over. After returning from Europe he was running a kitchen right here in Portland, at one of the city's better establishments. One night, Uncle Billy, just back from Memphis, literally burst through the restaurant's back door. He looked wild-eyed. Jonny figured he was hungry and threw a steak on the fire for him.

Billy waved the steak away, which got Jonny worried. Figuring his uncle was sick, he sat Billy down on a stool near the spice rack and got him a cold beer, which Billy didn't wave away. It revived him enough so that he could tell Jonny about the pork shoulder sandwiches.

You see, Uncle Billy loves to travel. He frequently buys a Greyhound ticket at the bus station in Portland and heads south for warmer weather, southern whiskey, ladies and barbeque. Although he's made the trip dozens of times, he had an idea during this one that had him rushing to the Memphis bus station anxious to see his nephew, but first he filled a good-sized sack with pork sandwiches.

His idea was that his nephew should open a restaurant that just served pork shoulder barbeque. McBilly's, he thought, would be the McDonald's of pork shoulder; folks could drive up, order pork sandwiches, coleslaw and beer and be on their way. His original plan was to give Jonny an example to work from, which is what the sack of sandwiches was about, but somewhere around Albany, right where the New York Thruway meets the Interstate, Uncle Billy succumbed to the aroma of barbeque and the last sandwich disappeared. He did, however, save the bag, which he gave to his nephew, suggesting that he work off the scent that still lingered on the brown paper.

Although not enthused by the prospect of owning a one-stop pork sandwich shop, but hoping to please his uncle's gastronomic craving, Jonny got right to work on the project. He fabricated a smoker out of a metal barrel, put it in a woodless woodshed he had out back at home and tacked the paper bag on the wall for inspiration. Every now and again Uncle Billy dropped by Jonny's impromptu smokehouse to encourage his nephew and sample his progress.

While coming up with the right combination of spices and smoke, Jonny's culinary inquisitiveness had discovered a new frontier. Each night at work he put on his kitchen whites with less enthusiasm. He began waking up earlier in the morning to have more time in his smokehouse. Uncle Billy's idea for a pork sandwich shop was, in Jonny's mind, developing into something more interesting — a barbeque joint in coastal Maine.

The pork that Jonny uses is called a Boston butt, which, despite its name, is actually a portion of the hog's shoulder. In the South this cut of meat is simply called shoulder. The 3½ to 4-pound shoulders that Jonny recommends you buy usually have less fat than other sizes of the same cut.

Down South, plain white bread is used for barbeque. Jonny prefers to use French or Italian breads. In barbeque, bread serves three main functions: to hold a sandwich together, to sop up gravy, to clean your hands by rolling it between your palms. The first time Killer Gene ate at Uncle Billy's he commented, "The bread's too good. Don't you folks in Maine have Wonder bread?"

Pulled and chopped and made into sandwiches, a cut this size will feed eight hungry people.

- 1 3½ to 4-pound pork butt
- 2 Tablespoons Sebago Pig & Poultry Rub
- 8 large hamburger-type rolls
- Killer Gene's Tar Heel Vinegar Sauce
- barbeque sauce
- 2 handfuls soaked wood or corn cob chips

Get your chips soaking at least two hours before starting out. Then build a medium-hot fire in your grill. Rub all sides of the shoulder with Sebago Pig & Poultry Rub, and set it, fat-side up, over an indirect heat on which you've just sprinkled a small handful of chips. Cover and cook for 4½ - 5 hours. Check the fire every couple of hours and add more chips and charcoal to keep the temperature medium-hot.

When the pork shoulder's internal temperature reaches 190°F, remove it from the grill and cool awhile. The meat will make a hollow hissing sound as you handle it. Put on a pair of heavy rubber gloves, the kind your oil deliveryman wears, locate and pull out the only bone remaining in the shoulder — a small piece of shoulder blade — and put it aside to use for stock in next week's jambalaya. If the meat has been properly cooked, the bone will pull out without a struggle.

Continue to pull apart the cooked shoulder with a fork and your gloved hands, then roughly chop the meat with a cleaver. This is what we mean by *pulled and chopped.*

Pile the pork onto rolls, or Wonder bread, squirt on some Killer Gene's Tar Heel Vinegar Sauce and a little barbeque sauce (or serve them on the side if you'd rather), and serve with a side order of Mother's Mountain Coleslaw, a heaping ladleful of Barbeque Billy Beans and a bowl of pickles.

Bastid Spare Ribs

When Jonny first opened Uncle Billy's, he cooked, waited on tables, washed dishes and tried his best at balancing the checkbook. As closing time neared, especially on Thursday nights, the noise coming through the wall separating Uncle Billy's from the bar next door would get loud. There'd be thumping, laughter, even applause in between verses of "Wild Colonial Boy," Uncle Billy's favorite Irish dirge. The baritone leading the barroom choir was, of course, Uncle Billy himself.

He hardly ever finished the song. He and a few buddies would slip out and three seconds later Billy would be at Jonny's doorway bellowing, "St. Laurent, you French bastid, are the ribs ready yet?"

It didn't take Jonny long to catch on. He'd bung four racks onto the barrel cooker as soon as the boys next door reached the first chorus. It didn't take customers long to catch on either, they started ordering their ribs bastid too.

- 2 racks pork spare ribs (with the rib-end trimmings)
- 1½ cups Georges Henri's Homebrew Barbeque Baste
- 4 Tablespoons Sebago Pig & Poultry Rub
- 1/2 cup barbeque sauce
- 3 handfuls soaked chips; hardwood and alder mix

If your butcher has trimmed the rack, make sure to rub, cook and baste the rib-end trimmings with the racks. If you're doing the trimming, leave the ends on the rack while you cook, and trim them before serving.

Get your wood chips in water and let them soak at least two

hours while you're preparing the ribs and fire.

Rub the Sebago Pig & Poultry Rub into the meaty side of the ribs, massaging it in well, then wrap the ribs in plastic wrap. Put the rubbed and wrapped ribs in the refrigerator and let them set while you get the grill going.

Prepare a medium-hot fire.

After the ribs have spent an hour in the refrigerator, take them out and put them bone-side down (the massaged and meaty side up) on the grill over an indirect heat that has been generously spread with chips. Remember to throw on the rib-end trimmings and close up the grill, keeping the dampers open just a crack. Keeping the dampers mostly closed creates a small amount of steaming, which makes for a wetter rib.

They'll cook for four or five hours. After two hours brush on a liberal amount of the baste, add more chips and charcoal and cover it back up.

ABOUT BASTING

Basting results in what are referred to as wet ribs, as opposed to dry, or unbasted. While this may seem a minor point, proponents of one type or another have been known to come to blows defending their preference. Dry rib aficionados rub but don't baste the ribs. Nephew Jonny knows better, however, and is happily ensconced in the *wet* camp.

After another hour give the ribs one more liberal basting. Don't waste your time flipping them over or moving them around; baste them, leave them alone and cover them again.

A meat thermometer stuck into the thickest, meatiest part of the rack after four hours of cooking, should read at least 195°F. If you don't have a meat thermometer yet cut into the rack. It should be pink around the edges. If not, you'll need to cook them a bit longer.

Once done, take the ribs off the grill and set them on a piece of foil just big enough to loosely envelop each rack. Slather each side with a good amount of the baste and then with barbeque sauce. Wrap them loosely in the foil, and put the racks back on the grill meaty side up, setting them directly over the coals. Cover the grill and cook for 15 minutes or so. Be extra careful at this point not to burn the ribs. If you have to, move the ribs around the grill to find the safest hot spot.

These ribs can be prepared days in advance of serving. If that's your pleasure, wrap them tight in foil after you take the ribs off the grill and refrigerate. The next day, or the day after, they'll just need a half an hour of indirect heat over a medium-hot fire to get them ready for eating.

A rib diner at Uncle Billy's includes Barbeque Billy Beans and Mother's Mountain Coleslaw on the side, and some cornbread to sop up the juices.

About those rib-end trimmings you tossed on the grill with the ribs; read on.

Uncle Billy at 15.
"Bill Hoadley is far out front in the Greater Portland
Junior Legion Baseball League batting race...the
15-year-old catcher-outfielder has nine hits in 17
at-bats for a .529 average. Hoadley is also tops
in base hits, triples and total bases."

— Portland Press Herald, *July 23, 1950*

Rib End Sandwiches

In barbeque, bread is more of a plate cleaner than a food holder. With Pork Shoulder Sandwich being the exception, serve a barbeque sandwich open by piling the meat on a single slice of bread. Rib ends, brisket, beef and pork tenderloin are eaten with fingers and forks, tearing off pieces of bread as you go. Backwoods Bourbon Whole-Log Arkansas Round Steak and Rib End Sandwiches are not traditional barbeque fare, so on those we break with tradition and put a second slice of bread on top.

- cooked rib-end trimmings*
- barbeque sauce
- pork stock or water
- 1 teaspoon granulated garlic
- 1 teaspoon black pepper
- 1 teaspoon salt

*See Bastid Spare Ribs

Rib End Sandwiches uses the trash-rib trimmings that you or your butcher whopped off the bastid rib racks. Assuming that you cooked and basted the rib-end trimmings along with the bastid ribs, here is what to do with the parts.

Get out your heavy rubber gloves and pull all the meat from the bones while the rib ends are still hot from the grill. Toss the meat onto a cutting board and chop it up with a cleaver. Set the bones to boiling for use in a soup stock.

Put the chopped and pulled meat in a heavy enamel or steel sauce pan and add enough barbeque sauce to cover. Dilute this with a small amount of pork stock or water, add the garlic, black pepper and salt. Bring to a simmer and cook, covered, for 30 minutes, stirring from time to time with a wooden spoon. Allow to cool, then store in the refrigerator until you're ready to use it. (We're assuming you'd rather eat the spare ribs today and the trimmings tomorrow.)

Napkin art no. 123

When you're ready to make Rib End Sandwiches, put some of the rib-end concoction into the microwave or a skillet on the stove and cook until hot. Put the sauced meat on bread or a bun and serve.

Uncle Billy has Jonny put large amounts of this Rib End Sandwich mixture into canning jars, for both his own personal consumption, and to give as Christmas gifts to his older girlfriends, the ones who'll mention him kindly in their wills.

Pork Tenders

Pork Tenders are easy to cook and tasty to eat, and are especially good when you're short on time and long on hunger.

- 1-pound pork tenderloin, peeled (fat removed)
- 2 ounces Apple Jack brandy (or Calvados)
- 1/4 teaspoon cloves
- 1 teaspoon black peppercorns, fresh cracked
- 1 Tablespoon Mother's Mountain Mustard (or other fine Dijon-style mustard)
- 1 handful of soaked fruitwood chips

Peel the membrane from the tenderloin. Start at the tail end of the tenderloin and work toward the head, pulling the thin membrane away from the meat. Also, pull away any clumps of fat at the head. If the membrane or fat won't let go, use a sharp knife. Use the flat side of a broad knife, a mortar and pestle or coffee grinder, to crack the peppercorns. Combine the Apple Jack, cloves and peppercorns, and rub it into the pork. Use the freshly cracked peppercorns right away, there's nothing like fresh cracked peppercorns. Next, slather on half of the mustard.

Get your grill to medium-hot. Sear the meat on all sides, then sprinkle the soaked chips onto the coals; move the pork to an indirect heat and cover, keeping the grill's dampers wide open. Cook for 15 minutes, slather on the rest of the mustard, cover again and cook another 15 minutes, or until the meat's internal temperature reaches 145°F, which is when the smell is about to drive you and your guests over the brink of decorum.

Remove the meat from the grill, let stand a minute or two, then slice thinly and serve, with Smoky Potatoes, maybe some Damn Good Sweet Onions and Vermont cider jelly as a condiment.

This will serve four people. If you have any leftovers, and it's worth making too much to get some, turn them into Bus Station Saigon Sandwiches.

Uncle Billy's Southside Barbeque,
with Elvis and the restrooms, Soo
and Wee, in the background.

Bus Station Saigon Sandwiches

One day, while waiting for Jonny to pick him up at the bus depot after a Greyhound excursion, Uncle Billy, wanting to get in from the rain, was attracted by some delectable smells downwind. He followed his nose across the street into a tiny Vietnamese restaurant called Saigon Sandwich, owned and operated by the ever-friendly Mme. Vinh Thi Bogalawski. It has become a favorite haunt of Billy's, who always picks up a couple of sandwiches for bus rides north and south.

Jonny recreates this dish using the leftovers from Pork Tenders as the main ingredient, which is what we're suggesting here. Truth be told, Billy and Jonny prefer going to the Saigon Sandwich for these sandwiches and a side of fiery hot kim-chee (gimchee).

- 1 good crusty French baguette roll per sandwich, sliced lengthwise and heated
- 3-4 ounces cold pork tenderloin per sandwich, sliced paper-thin
- fresh carrot, grated
- Thai peppers (very hot), rough chopped
- cucumber, peeled and sliced thin
- fresh cilantro, stalks and all, unchopped
- pork or chicken liver pate (Vietnamese if you can get it)
- shallots, rough chopped, sauteed until translucent in a mixture of sesame oil and butter

☞ **Mme. Vinh Thi Bogalawski's Sauce**
(This will make enough sauce for three or four sandwiches.)
- 2 Tablespoons Vietnamese hot chili garlic sauce
- 1 Tablespoon fresh-squeezed lime juice
- 1 Tablespoon sugar
- 3 Tablespoons noc-cham (Fish Sauce)

Despite the inflammatory nature of these ingredients, and casting aside the advice of Uncle Billy's internist at Maine Medical Center, they combine to make one terrific sandwich. According to Uncle Billy, Bus Station Saigon Sandwiches are the single most appropriate resting place for good, smoked Pork Tenders. And who are we to disagree?

Napkin art no. 621

To construct a Bus Station Saigon Sandwich, slice open a French roll, leaving the ends intact to form a pocket in the middle, in which to deposit the meat and such. Put all the sandwich ingredients into the roll. The order doesn't matter, but generally speaking put pate, pork and shallots in first and then pile on the veggies.

To make the sauce, combine the ingredients and stir well, then pour judiciously over the sandwich's filling. The key to the sandwich's heat is the chili garlic sauce. Increase or decrease the amount according to your own fortitude.

Jonny always drinks a sweetened soy milk with his sandwich, while Uncle Billy usually brings his own beverage. When Jonny's boys are with them, they like to have egg rolls with their sandwiches.

Backwoods Bourbon
Whole-Log Arkansas Round Steak

Uncle Billy, as much a stranger to temperance as Carrie Nation was a friend to it, found himself coming off a week-long celebration in the fair town of Memphis, Tennessee, when he happened upon an early morning eating establishment. Inside, he found an oddity on the menu, or at least an item unknown to him called Arkansas Round Steak. He pondered the possible ramifications of such a dish but, trusting that no good Memphis barbeque joint could possibly serve anything objectionable, he ordered up a plate. What Uncle Billy got, simply put, was a bun full of smoked bologna with a topping of Vidalia onions.

Napkin art no. 156

Uncle Billy, never one to hide his feelings, laughed out loud at the meal set in front of him. But after a couple of bites, he found himself ordering a second round, and soon after that, a third. Billy knows a good thing when he bites into it.

Back home in Maine, Uncle Billy had the usual thought that comes to most Mainers, which is, "What they can do good, we can do better." What follows is a combination of Yankee ingenuity, Kentucky sour mash and Memphis barbeque. We'll get to the sour mash in a minute; in the meantime, find some chipped corn cobs or alderwood for the smoke, and some fair-enough bourbon for the soaking.

- 1, 4-5 pound bologna log, 4-5 inches in diameter
- 1 bottle bourbon
- 1 handful chips (corn cob or alder wood if they're around), soaked in sour mash bourbon/water mix
- 1 pound sweet Vidalia onions, cut into thin rounds or 1 quart coleslaw
- hamburger rolls
- barbeque sauce

Soak the chips for a few hours in one-part bourbon and four-parts water. Place the bologna log over an indirect medium-hot fire, to which the soaked cob or wood chips have just been added. Close the lid immediately so none of that good whiskey smoke disappears.

Bologna comes already cooked so there's no reason to be poking your nose in the cooker. Stay away and let the bologna smoke. This is where the sour mash comes in. Sit back and do like Billy does, which is to sample the bourbon while the bologna sucks up all that good smoke.

After an hour, take the bologna off the grill and slice it into thin rounds with a sharp knife. Throw it on board a bun, top it off with the thin-sliced Vidalias or coleslaw. Put the barbeque sauce on the table, leaving its use up to everyone's own preference.

What you do with the rest of the bourbon is your business. But if there is any bologna left over, put it in the refrigerator. Jonny sends it off in his kid's lunch boxes, and he himself has been known to have a slice or two late at night. It also jazzes up a Lutheran bean supper casserole, macaroni and cheese, jambalaya, chili or split pea soup.

POULTRY

Judge D.T. Child's Smoked Cornish Game Hens
with Buttermilk and Cranberry

·

Barbequed Chicken

·

Voodoo Jerk Chicken

Uncle Billy can be counted on to show up at the back door each and every night at 9 o'clock, looking for an order of barbequed chicken and a double side of Barbeque Billy Beans. Sometimes he varies it just a little and takes ribs or a little brisket for his evening meal, though his first love is still the chicken Jonny and his crew barbeque out back in Oprah, the double barreled wood-fired cooker.

One well-known restaurant reviewer, obviously pleased with what proved to be the first of many visits to Uncle Billy's Barbeque, said of his chicken dinner, "It was so succulent and tender that a harsh word would make the meat fall off the bone." Fine words about a fine meal, and a fitting epitaph for many a good bird.

Soon-to-be-barbequed chickens hanging in Oprah, the double-barrel cooker, with racks of bastid spare ribs underneath. Jonny fuels Oprah with red oak, maple and alder when he can get it.

Rib Joint Juke Box

Rib joints without music are like ribs without sauce. After an exhaustive and unscientific study by what must have been a very bored Nephew Jonny, the following are the most-played songs on the juke box at Uncle Billy's. We're darned if we can make any sense of it. They are presented in no particular order, and since Jonny lost the napkin he made his notes on, they're more than likely to stay that way.

1. "A Tombstone Every Mile" by Dick Curless
2. "Papa Was A Rolling Stone" by The Temptations
3. "Beat Me Daddy, Eight to the Bar" by CommanderCody and His Lost Planet Airmen
4. "The Theme From Shaft" by Isaac Hayes
5. "Havah Nagilah" by The Arthur Lyman Group
6. "It's Not Unusual" by Tom Jones
7. "The Second Week of Deer Camp" by Da Yoopers
8. "These Boots Are Made for Walkin'" by Nancy Sinatra
9. "Won't Go Huntin' With You Jake, I'll Just Go Chasin' Women" by Jimmy Dean
10. "I'm A Hog For You" by The Surfaris
11. "Harper Valley P.T.A." by Jeannie C. Riley
12. "The Good, The Bad and The Ugly" by Hugo Montenegro

Judge D.T. Child's Smoked Cornish Game Hens with Buttermilk and Cranberry

This recipe probably wouldn't exist had there been more ducks, one chilly autumn afternoon a couple of years back. The way the quite-Honorable Judge D.T. Child settled a family dispute involving two of Uncle Billy's cousins and a traveling rock band so impressed Billy and Jonny, they invited him on a duck hunting weekend the next fall. They had such a good time they spend a four-day weekend together every duck season.

One fall, for reasons probably known only to the ducks, what few ducks there were didn't move, except to bob on the swells. To warm themselves at the end of that long, cold, foggy, duckless day, the Judge and Billy sent Jonny down to the Pond Cove agency store for some restorative spirits. While there he picked up a couple of game hens and fixed them up that night the same as he would have fixed the ducks they wound up not shooting. Needless to say, this recipe is mighty fine when you use it with game hens, but also works well with duck.

This recipe will feed four normal people, or three failed hunters.

- 2 Rock Cornish game hens, split in half lengthwise
- 8 ounces cranberries
- 1/4 cup Barbados molasses
- 2 Tablespoons shallots, finely chopped
- 3 ounces blackberry brandy
- 2 heaping teaspoons cornstarch
- 1 teaspoon dried chervil leaves
- 1/4 teaspoon grated mace
- 1/4 teaspoon ground nutmeg
- pinch of sage
- 1/2 cup buttermilk
- 1 ounce rum, light or dark
- 2 Tablespoons margarine
- 1 walnut-size piece of sweet butter
- salt and pepper to taste

Combine the cranberries with the molasses and shallots in a heavy saucepan. Do not cover; stir often and bring to a boil.

Meanwhile, in a small bowl combine the blackberry brandy with the cornstarch and a pinch of salt, and mix into the cranberries. Cook and stir another five minutes, until the cranberry mixture looks thickened, then set it on the back porch to cool.

In another bowl, combine the spices with the buttermilk and rum. Stir thoroughly and then set aside.

Rub the softened margarine on the outside of the hens and season both sides with salt and pepper.

Sear the birds skin side down over direct heat on a very hot grill. This will only take a few minutes. Once they're seared jerk them over and arrange your grill so that a drip pan is positioned between the coals and under the hens. The pan will catch the drippings, which will be used later. Before closing the grill lid, liberally baste the birds with the buttermilk mixture and cook them over this indirect heat for about 25 minutes. Baste periodically — every five minutes is about right.

Remove the birds from the grill to a serving platter and place in a warming oven. Bring in the cranberries and get the drippings from the grill. Combine the drippings with the remainder of the buttermilk baste and reduce, in a saucepan, over a high heat. When the sauce is thick enough to coat your spoon, add the sweet butter and stir. Pour half of the sauce over the birds and serve the rest on the side, preferably with warm French bread and a tumbler of that smooth single-malt Scotch whiskey the Judge keeps locked in his study.

Barbequed Chicken

Down behind Uncle Billy's Barbeque, Nephew Jonny works every day in a converted steel sugar shack where he has a nine-foot tall metal double-barrel cooker with about 75 hooks in it. Jonny hangs halved chickens on these hooks and cooks them over red oak. Awful hot work in August, damned chilly about mid-February but Jonny claims to enjoy it, or at least he pretends to.

Here's a recipe that doesn't take quite as much dedication to the out-of-doors, but still gives you a chicken "like you ain't ever had nowhere before."

- 2 3½ to 4-pound split broiler chickens
- 1 heaping Tablespoon Sebago Pig & Poultry Rub
- 1 small handful of soaked chips

Purchase whole chickens and ask the butcher to split them with his bandsaw. When picking out chicken, try to avoid the ones with bright yellow skins. They may look better, but chickens don't come by yellow skin naturally so you're better off spending a little less for a paler bird.

Rub the inside of the chicken halves with the Sebago Pig & Poultry Rub, salt and pepper. If there's any rub left on your hands when you're done, rub it on the chicken's skin. Wrap the chicken halves in plastic wrap, put in the refrigerator and let them sit overnight. Soak some fruitwood or corn cob chips overnight as well.

The next day, build a medium-hot to hot grill, remove the wrap and place the chickens, skin-side down, on the grill directly over the coals. Sear the chickens for two minutes and then jerk them over to an indirect heat, skin-side up and cover, with the damper vents half-open. Cook for two hours, at which time you'll be able to twist the drumstick at the joint and it will separate easily, without a crack. The meat will appear pink, but that's normal for barbeque cooking. To double check, jab a fork into the thickest part of a thigh. The juice that flows should be clear. The internal temperature of the cooked chicken should be 185°F on your cooking thermometer.

Napkin art no. 69

While some recipes call for slathering all manner of syrups, sauces and gyppos on the birds while they cook, Jonny prefers to serve them at the table. In real life, barbeque sauce doesn't adhere to chicken the way it does on TV commercials, but it does adhere to the grill. Rather than scrape the mess off the grill, serve the chicken with barbeque sauce on the side, coleslaw and Billy Beans.

Voodoo Jerk Chicken

Uncle Billy found Voodoo Jerk Slather Sauce while in the Caribbean, at a little beach-front restaurant that doubled late at night as a sort of Moose Lodge for ceremonial rites. At a key point in one of the ceremonies Billy was invited to attend, a green, almost phosphorescent sauce was slathered onto the fish and poultry that the islanders were cooking and jerking around on a large, primitive grill. The aroma was unlike anything Billy had ever experienced. It made his eyes smart and parched his lips.

Determined to find out more about this sauce, he decided to teach a West Indian voodoo chef a game of cards. Uncle Billy, with designs on the recipe, also shared a significant portion of a couple bottles of rum with the yellow-eyed chef. Successful at poker, he brought the recipe back home to Maine, where Nephew Jonny gave a try at making it. His efforts were stymied at first, because one of the most important ingredients in jerk sauce is the Scotch Bonney pepper, an item in short supply at the corner market. Imagine Jonny's surprise, when he found a group of local gardeners happy to grow them for him, and then a green grocer in Puerto Rico who ships him all he needs when the local supplies fall short.

Every few weeks Jonny makes up a new batch of his Voodoo Jerk Slather Sauce. The neighbors don't need to ask what day he'll be cooking up a batch, they just sniff the air and if their eyes start to water they know the answer. Then they head straight for Uncle Billy's for a plateful of Voodoo Jerk Chicken.

- 2 3½ to 4-pound split broiler chickens
- 2 Tablespoons Voodoo Jerk Slather Sauce
- 1/8 teaspoon salt
- 1/8 teaspoon black pepper
- 1 handful soaked corn cob, alder or fruitwood chips

Rub the insides of the chicken halves with Voodoo Jerk Slather Sauce. Keeping the skin as intact as possible, slather more sauce under the skin. This jerk sauce is more than hot, it's about two degrees left of spontaneous combustion, so you might consider wearing rubber gloves. Whatever you do, don't get it on any sensitive parts of your body that you might care to use later.

Wrap the birds in plastic wrap, put them in the refrigerator and let them sit overnight. Soak some fruitwood or corn cob chips overnight, and if you can find some alderwood, that's even better.

To cook, turn back one recipe and follow the directions for Barbeque Chicken. If you marinated the slathered chicken over-night, cut the cooking time by 30 minutes. Yes, that's right, the refrigerator is no match for the heat generated by Uncle Billy's Voodoo Jerk Slather Sauce.

This method of marinating overnight in the refrigerator followed by a smoky slow cook allows the flavor of the sauce and smoke to fully penetrate the meat. Try serving the chicken with some more of the Voodoo Jerk Slather Sauce if you're up to it, and Uncle Billy's Own Barbeque Sauce on the side. A cold brewed beverage or two would not be considered a distraction. In fact, it might be a neces-sity. If your mouth is burning, but you can't stop eating the chicken, you did everything just right.

BEEF

Brisket and Burnt Ends
·
Cousin Kim's Gimchee Short Ribs
·
Dinosaur Bone Slow Cook Beef Back Rib
·
Marcel's Grilled and Smoked Tenderloin of Beef
·
Flank Steak Weekend

When Jonny first opened Uncle Billy's Barbeque, beef wasn't on the menu. There was pork, chicken and fish, but no beef. People — expatriate Texans and beef-loving Yankees — kept asking for it, though, and eventually Jonny found himself working on his first brisket recipes. These days, the part-time embalmer and the vegetarian truck driver who help Jonny in the smokehouse are hard-pressed to make enough, even with the cooker cranking six days a week.

A good place to look for fresh brisket is at Jewish markets, where it is consistently available. Elsewhere brisket is routinely corned, which is not what you want. When ordering, tell the butcher you want a trimmed Choice beef brisket, hold the corn. Make sure to specify that you want an aged Choice brisket, which assures your final product will be tender and flavorful. Have the butcher trim the excess fat, but not all of it. Even a trimmed brisket will have a fairly substantial layer of fat left on top. You'll trim that later, just don't bother putting a lot of Heifer Pat Down on the fatty portion.

The culinary technique used in barbequing cuts of meat like brisket is a braising process, where the internal fat roasts the meat from within as it soaks up the smoke from without. The result will be spectacular as long as you follow the golden rule of barbeque: Cook it low and slow. Brisket cooked too fast will be dry and slice like a pot roast. A properly cooked brisket will be moist and, when sliced across the grain, internally will have at least a half-inch thick perimeter of pink *ring of smoke* underneath its blackened, whooped-out looking exterior. No self respecting barbequer would serve anything less.

The best bet is to set up your lounge chair, pick up a good book or turn on the television, and settle in for the long haul. Trust us; it's worth it in the end.

Few cuts of beef lend themselves to slow-cook barbeque like short ribs, back ribs and brisket. Despite Ranger Mel's advice, early on Jonny used more expensive cuts of beef, but he just wound up wasting a lot of money. Jonny should have listened to Mel, and we suggest you listen to Jonny — unless of course you have a bunch of money to throw away.

One of those more expensive cuts, skirt steak, cut from beneath the prime rib, is well marbled and particularly flavorful, and does better on the grill when cooked over a direct heat. Tenderloin is a lean cut and also requires quick cooking over a direct heat. Left on the fire too long and tenderloin becomes tough-loin.

Uncle Billy, guarding the brisket.

Brisket and Burnt Ends

The only thing that spends more time in the cooker than Nephew Jonny is Nephew Jonny's brisket of beef. In fact, next to whole hogs and sides of beef, nothing cooks longer and slower than the brisket he prepares at Uncle Billy's restaurant.

If you have friends from Texas, where they love their brisket, by all means invite them over, but don't let them give you any lip about only using mesquite wood. Living here in Maine, a state that has more trees than even the paper companies know what to do with, it seems downright silly to import desert shrubbery.

Jonny uses whole red oak logs in his big cooker and, sometimes, mesquite charcoal (not fresh mesquite wood) at home. If there aren't any trees where you live, or if you'd rather have mesquite, Kingsford makes a good charcoal briquet with chips of mesquite wood in it. You can also buy bags of chipped mesquite at some supermarkets, many kitchen stores and mail order catalogs (see Where to Buy Barbeque Stuff). If you prefer, you can also buy bags of mesquite charcoal through the mail.

This recipe, using a medium-size brisket, will serve six.

- 6 - 7 pound fresh brisket of Choice beef
- 1/4 cup Jonny's Heifer Pat Down
- 2 teaspoons salt
- 2 teaspoons pepper
- 3 handfuls soaked hardwood chips, or mesquite charcoal
- Blackburn's Maple Barbeque Sauce

When preparing a brisket for barbeque, remove just enough of the fat to clean it up a bit, and it's ready to rub. Save the suet trimmings to put in the birds' suet feeder.

While building a medium-hot fire, rub in the Heifer Pat Down, salt and pepper real good on all but the fatty side of the meat. When the fire's ready throw the chips over the coals. Then put the brisket on the grill fatty-side up, over indirect heat so it cooks real slow. Cover the grill and let it sit for two hours, which is when you'll have to add more charcoal and chips.

Peek in every once in a while to make sure the fire hasn't gone out. The objective here is to keep the heat and the smoke consistent throughout cooking. As the fat renders and drops down, the grill has potential for a real conflagration. Be sure to keep an eye on the grill and the spritzer handy.

The brisket will be ready in five hours, but if you have the time, let it go another hour. The brisket is ready when its internal temperature reaches 190°F.

The beef will finish out at half its original size, and will be pretty black and whooped-out looking. That's perfect with brisket — the nastier looking the better.

To serve, pull the ends off and slice the meat across the grain. This sounds easy, but you'll find that the grain changes direction. It'll get easier with a little practice. Always use a sharp serrated knife.

Brisket serves up nice on a slice of Jalapeno Cheesebread with barbeque sauce on the side.

The brisket's burnt ends, which are exactly what they sound like, are considered choice pickings and at some barbeque establishments, most notably in Kansas City, they are served as an appetizer. Jonny prefers to serve the ends in with slices of brisket. But at your house you can do as you please, as long as you cook it low and slow.

Cousin Kim's Gimchee Short Ribs

Somewhere on the other side of the ocean Uncle Billy has a friend he refers to as Cousin Kim. They met in the early Fifties when Billy was on a government-sponsored trip to Korea. He eventually returned to Maine with both his health and his appetite intact. The former he says he owes to the advice his mother gave him, which was "Keep your head down!" The latter he said was due to the fine food Cousin Kim made for him at a small restaurant on the outskirts of Seoul.

The meaty short ribs used here are the cut of choice for many Korean dishes. The ribs are not only barbequed, they are also braised so the meat falls off the bone when it is done.

Allow about a half-pound per person. This recipe serves four.

- 2 pounds short ribs of beef
- 1/4 cup soy sauce
- 1/4 cup Hoisin sauce or ketchup
- 1 ounce cheap Scotch whiskey
- 1 Tablespoon fresh ginger, peeled and finely chopped
- 2 cloves fresh garlic, mashed and finely chopped
- 1 teaspoon Schechuan hot oil
- 1 teaspoon black pepper
- 1 teaspoon sesame oil with 2 Tablespoons peanut oil
- 1 handful corn cob or hardwood chips
- 1 heaping Tablespoon cornstarch
- 1 Tall Boy (16 ounces) can of beer or beef stock
- chopped scallions for garnish

Combine all ingredients, except the beer, oil, cornstarch and scallions, in a shallow dish. With a sharp knife, score the pieces of meat 1/4-inch deep in a grid pattern. Refrigerate the ribs in the marinade for anywhere from an hour to a day, turning them occasionally.

When ready to cook, remove the ribs from the marinade (setting aside the marinade for later) and brush them with the sesame and peanut oil mixture.

Put the short ribs directly over the coals of a medium-hot grill. Sear one minute each side using a pair of long-handled tongs to flip them. If the meat sticks to the grill the fire isn't hot enough. Toss the water-soaked corn cobs or wood chips on the fire, move the ribs to an indirect heat and cover.

Leave the ribs to smoke for 1½ to 2 hours, during which time you could drive downtown to buy a pint of gimchee if you want to do some interesting things to your palate; or coleslaw if you want to play it safe. Here in Portland we're fortunate to have a number of good Korean and Oriental markets, many of which serve up mighty potent gimchee.

The ribs should look charred but not burnt when you take them off the grill. Then put them in a heavy skillet or Dutch oven, sprinkle on the cornstarch, pour in the reserved marinade and the beer and, watching closely so it doesn't scorch, simmer the ribs on the stove, uncovered, flipping them around a couple of times. Keep it up for 15-20 minutes over a low heat. You'll wind up with a gravy like no other. Uncle Billy likes to pour the gravy over baked potatoes. Serve with the fiery gimchee and big pitchers of beer on the side, which was how Uncle Billy and Cousin Kim ate this meal.

Dinosaur Bone Slow-Cook Beef Back Ribs

Uncle Billy's great uncle, Great-Uncle Billy, spent a good chunk of the Spanish-American War sleeping, crawling and lying wounded on the ground just outside of Amarillo, Texas. In doing so he acquired a taste for beef ribs that must have infiltrated his genes. He left Texas somewhere around the turn of the century and never went back, though he would have had an invite been sent.

So as a salute to Great-Uncle Billy in particular, and to Texas in general, here is his favorite slow-cook rib preparation.

You'll feed four with this.

- 5 pounds choice beef back ribs
- 10 ounces Uncle Billy's Heifer Pat-Down (2-oz. per pound)
- 2 teaspoons salt
- 2 teaspoons pepper
- 3 handfuls soaked corn cobs, hardwood chips, or mesquite charcoal

Vigorously rub the spice mix into the meaty side of the ribs. Wrap in plastic film and refrigerate overnight; or rub, wrap and put them outside on a hot day for a couple of hours. This won't hurt the beef ribs one bit — as long as you don't overdo it. Either way gets the spice mixture worked in real nice. Soak the wood chips a couple hours before starting the fire.

One advantage to using back ribs (beef or pork) is that they stand up to higher temperatures than side or spare ribs, which makes them better for grilling directly over the coals.

When the ribs are ready, scatter half the soaked wood chips around the inside of a medium-low grill. Place the ribs on the grill, bone-side down, cover, and sit back and forget about them for an hour. Then scatter in the rest of the wood chips, add more charcoal and close the lid again quickly so the good smells don't make you drool on the meat. Close the vents almost completely down. Now, go make yourself busy for another 60 minutes or so.

After two hours of cooking, the internal temperature of the thickest part of the meat should be 150 to 160°F; if it is below this keep cooking, otherwise remove the ribs from the grill and set aside.

Build up the fire to medium-hot, place the ribs back on the grill, but not directly over the hot coals and cover, leaving the vents half-open. Give them 45 minutes or so, at which point you should easily be able to tear them apart with your hands if you're wearing your heavy rubber gloves. The internal temperature of the thick pieces will be 185 to 190°F. They will look slightly pink inside, and the surface will be charred but not burned. That's done. Remove them from the grill, cut into portions or individual ribs and serve.

It's party time. Grandmother Alice, Jonny and
Uncle Billy at Jonny's first birthday.

Marcel's Grilled and Smoked Tenderloin of Beef

While Jonny was cooking for Marcel at the Samoset Resort, mid-coast Maine's only four-star resort, Uncle Billy drove to Rockport to help Jonny tend the grill for a big party. That night, Maine got hit with its worst snowstorm in 50 years. The only person to arrive that evening, aside from the restaurant staff, was Billy.

Marcel and Billy hit it right off. As the snowflakes fell, they swapped stories and feasted on this tenderloin preparation.

Marcel, besides being one of Jonny's all-time favorite chefs and mentor, was a man who could eat an entire tenderloin by himself, as long as he had sufficient quantities of vintage Bordeaux to wash it down.

Provided that your own appetite is of less heroic proportions, this recipe will serve six.

- 1 4-5 pound whole Choice tenderloin of beef, peeled
- 3 ounces any kind of vodka
- 2 ounces Jonny's Heifer Pat Down
- 1 teaspoon salt
- 1 teaspoon pepper
- 2 Tablespoons margarine

Rub down the tenderloin with a liberal amount of vodka, then rub in the Pat Down, salt and pepper. Wrap it in plastic wrap and put in the refrigerator overnight.

On eating day get the grill going hot. While it's heating up, melt the margarine in a small pan or microwave. Right before you put the tenderloin on the grill, slather the margarine on the meat with your hand or a brush — hand is better.

Flip the meat until all surfaces are seared; 30 seconds on each side should be enough. (You'll find that long-handled tongs will keep your hands from becoming barbeque during this part.) Then position the meat so that the thinner part is over an indirect heat and the thickest section is over a direct fire, then cover the grill leaving the vents wide open.

It's all too easy to overcook a tenderloin, so be careful. Cook 10-15 minutes for medium rare, 20-25 minutes for well done, being sure to keep any flare-ups under control with your spritzer.

Remove from the grill and let the meat stand a couple of minutes. Then carve and serve at tableside, slicing the

Napkin art no. 29

tenderloin into half-inch slices across the grain. Damn Good Sweet Grilled Onions, chanterelles (or other wild mushrooms) that have been basted with melted butter and rolled about the grill for two or three minutes, and some of Joel's Quick Grilled Potatoes complement this gourmand repast. For dessert make a Death by Chocolate Sauce Souffle and serve with a snifter of Cognac. Marcel would.

Flank Steak Weekend

To tell the truth, Flank Steak Weekend doesn't have a thing to do with flank steak. As near as anyone can figure, it goes back to a weekend furlough Uncle Billy had when he was in basic training preparing to save the Free World from the Worldwide Spread of Godless Communism — or something like that. Billy is uncharacteristically vague about the details.

Whatever took place did so during a weekend furlough in a Tex-Mex border town known for its chocolate chili mole (pronounced mo-lay) sauce, and pretty women. He enjoyed the food, he enjoyed the women's company, and that's all he'll say.

The meat used in Flank Steak Weekend is actually skirt steak, which is cut from right below the prime rib. This cut of meat is rich and flavorful and is ideal cooked quickly on the grill. You can use flank steak if you prefer, but Jonny uses skirt steak because it works better.

This meal is so good you'll need to allow at least a half-pound of meat per person. We've got it figured for two here.

- 1-pound+ piece of skirt steak
- 1/2 teaspoon salt
- 1/2 teaspoon black pepper
- 1½ Tablespoons Uncle Billy's Chocolate Chipotle Mole Sauce
- 1 Tablespoon tequila (optional)
- Mesquite charcoal, or regular charcoal with soaked mesquite or hardwood chips

☞ **For the Mole Sauce**
- 1 ounce dried chipotle pepper soaked in 1 cup water for 2 hours, or a dried jalapeno
- 1 teaspoon ground coriander
- 1/8 teaspoon ground cinnamon
- 1 Tablespoon hazelnut butter
- 1 Tablespoon sesame butter, or tahini
- 1 teaspoon lard
- 1 clove fresh garlic

- pinch ground clove
- pinch black pepper
- 2 ounces bitter chocolate

To prepare the sauce, put all the ingredients into a blender or food processor and whiz until it forms a paste. Nephew Jonny makes his own Chocolate Mole Sauce, however commercial preparations are available at specialty food stores, health food stores, or shops specializing in Mexican or Tex-Mex foods. Actually, the hard part is finding the dried chipotle, which is a jalapeno pepper smoke-dried over a mesquite fire. The Pendery's catalog lists them.

Here's how Uncle Billy describes the rest of the meal's preparation: "Whang together the Pat Down and the Mole Sauce, and rub it all over the beef, workin' it in real, real good. Nothing to it." Billy's never been one for details.

If you've got the time to plan ahead, after you've whanged and rubbed the meat, wrap it in plastic wrap and let sit in the refrigerator overnight. Otherwise, give it at least an hour, whanged, rubbed and wrapped, in the refrigerator.

After it's set awhile, unwrap the meat and put it right on the grill over a medium-hot to hot fire and close the lid, leaving the vents wide open. After five minutes, turn the meat and cook for another five minutes. If, during cooking, the fire flares up, move the meat to another part of the grill. As a fire safety tip, Uncle Billy reminds us that tequila doesn't make for much of a fire extinguisher.

To serve, slice the meat across the grain as thinly as possible, just as you would London Broil. It's fine just like that, but here in Portland we've got some good Italian bakeries, so at Jonny's place he wraps fresh, crusty Italian bread around the meat and serves it with sliced onions, shredded lettuce, sliced radishes and pickled chili peppers.

LAMB

Dry Rub Lamb Riblets

•

Double-Cut Fireplace Lamb Chops

•

Quick Mesquite-Grilled Butterflied Leg of Lamb
with Classic English Mint Sauce

At one time, raising lamb, mutton and goat was a major industry throughout northern New England — Maine, New Hampshire and Vermont. By the turn of the last century, however, there was hardly a blueberry bush, wildflower or blade of field grass left standing, so intensive were the animals' grazing habits and so poor was the management of the land. As a result, the U.S. sheep-raising business pretty much pulled up stakes and headed west, where the plains still had cover and the hills still had forests.

Today, lamb has returned to New England. The land has had almost a century of rest, and a new breed of sheep farmer has taken up the tradition and is raising smaller flocks of good, quality lamb.

In New England, lamb often comes from a neighbor's farm after it has been milk-fed by its maamaa for a few months. Fresh lamb is usually available from just before Easter on through the summer months.

Over the course of a year Uncle Billy's Barbeque is called on to cater a lamb roast or three. When that occurs, off goes Nephew Jonny, with his motorized spit in tow, behind Melvin, the official Uncle Billy's vehicle, a somewhat dilapidated, brightly multi-colored GMC pickup truck with green day-glo polka dots.

Melvin and Jonny are quite a sight returning home from one of these roasts. Uncle Billy is often waiting to help Jonny unload in hopes that some choice morsel or two might still be warm. Billy often gives Jonny a hard time about his truck, but never about his lamb barbeque, "I've seen things that may have looked a sight sillier, but none that ever smelled better."

Eddie Griffin, Jonny's landlord and proprietor of the drinking establishment next door, just laughs and shakes his head. "I don't know what you're doing kid," he tells Jonny, "but you're putting on a helluva show."

Dry Rub Lamb Riblets

While on his annual bus tour to the bourbon distilleries of Tennessee, Uncle Billy made the mandatory Memphis stopover at Charlie Vergo's Rendezvous for a feast of lamb riblets. Charlie, being Greek, and Billy being a Mainer (a nationality unto itself), have at least one thing in common: they both like to sit down and eat lamb until they can't eat anymore. Visitors to Maine gravitate to L.L. Bean in Freeport like tongues to a cowlick; in Memphis they go to Charlie Vergos, even if it means passing up that third trip to Graceland.

On the bus ride back home, somewhere between Asheville and Portland, Billy had a barbeque-scented, bourbon-fueled gastronomic revelation. He says he saw, through his bus window, the Maine countryside whipping by. They turned a bend in the road past a rock-sloped hillside, and he saw a green field full of sheep, dotted with spring lambs. He spent the next minutes calculating how many ribs were grazing in that field.

Billy headed to his nephew's house directly from the bus station. The next day Jonny, inspired by his uncle, set to work on lamb riblets Uncle Billy style. To the delight of Uncle Billy and his friends, this recipe is the result of that work. We eat them as appetizers or as a meal. Allow one slab per person for a main course serving, more if they're particularly hungry.

This recipe serves two.

- 2 racks lamb loin ribs, 1 pound each (also known as Denver Ribs)
- 2 Tablespoons olive oil
- 1 cup dry white Greek Retsina or other dry white wine
- 2 heaping Tablespoons Ram Island Dry Lamb Rub
- 1/2 teaspoon salt
- 1/2 teaspoon pepper
- 2 handfuls Retsina-soaked fruitwood or corn cob chips

In a shallow dish, marinate the ribs in the oil and wine for at least an hour, longer if you have the time. After marinating, work the Rub well into the meaty side of the ribs. If you're good at planning ahead, wrap in plastic film and put the ribs in the refrigerator overnight to cure. If you're cooking today, go ahead and get the grill ready.

The addition of the Retsina-smoked corn cobs or fruitwood chips to the coals is Uncle Billy's contribution to these lamb riblets. While they're not necessary to the recipe, they add nicely to the flavor and the cooking aromas. Soak the chips for about two hours before using. You can, of course, soak them in water if that's your preference. Put half the chips on the coals just before you start cooking the ribs. Build the fire to medium-hot, lay the ribs over direct heat, meat-side up and close the grill, leaving the vents half-open.

Close your cooker but keep an eye on it, lest the ribs flare up. Keep your spritzer handy. If there seems to be a bit too much flame, move the riblets to a calmer part of the grill. Assuming you have the combustion under control, keep the ribs on the hot part of the grill for 10 minutes or so, then open the grill and move them to an indirect heat and add the second handful of chips. Close the grill, damp down the vents almost completely, then make yourself useful by uncorking and sampling some of those big bottles of cold Retsina you've been hiding in the ice box down-cellar.

The ribs cook slowly and it'll be a good hour and a half until they're ready. Check them with a meat thermometer to be sure; if it registers 120°F, they're ready. You can also tell they're done when you can easily break them apart with your hands (wearing your heavy rubber gloves).

Take the ribs off the grill, pour the wine, sprinkle a little more Lamb Rub on the hot meat and cut into individual ribs with a sharp knife (or serve racks and let your guests go to it with a steak knife). Nephew Jonny enjoys some Smoky Potatoes on the Grill with his riblets while Uncle Billy eats the ribs all by themselves, although he has been known to put a little of Uncle Billy's Own Barbeque Sauce on them. When Jonny serves these ribs, he puts Classic English Mint Sauce and a cruet of raspberry vinegar on the table.

Melvin at rest.

Double-Cut Fireplace Lamb Chops

You can cook this one in your fireplace. A backyard grill will work fine, but it won't be as cozy.

Get a few of those fish grilling racks you see in the L.L. Bean catalog and kitchen supply stores. They're not expensive, but are plenty useful, as you'll discover when the chops flare up in the first few moments of cooking and their long handles keep your hands out of the flames. You can use them later to cook fish on the grill when the bluefish are running.

Since the fireplace is conducive to romantic notions, the portions figured here are for just two. Open a bottle of 1986 Craftsbury Pinot Noir, put a Tom Jones tape in the eight-track, and enjoy some good eats in a refined setting. (The candles on the ingredients list are for atmosphere, not eating.)

- 6 double-cut lamb loin chops (8-10 ounces per person)
- 4 cloves of garlic, finely minced
- 1/4 cup dry red wine (preferably a Burgundy)
- 3 Tablespoons olive oil
- 3 Tablespoons balsamic vinegar
- 3 Tablespoons rosemary leaves
- 1/2 teaspoon fresh-ground black pepper
- 1/2 teaspoon salt
- 2, 12-inch tapered candles, flickering seductively

Put all the ingredients — except the chops — into a shallow ceramic or glass casserole dish. Stir, and then add the chops, turning them three or four times to coat well. Leave the chops in the dish, cover with plastic film and put it in the refrigerator. Allow the chops to marinate for at least two hours, as long as overnight if you can, turning them once during this time.

Make a fire (remember, we're at the fireplace not the backyard grill) out of split, dry red oak or maple if you can get them. Apple and pear wood is also nice. When the fire has mostly turned to coals, remove the chops from the marinade and put them in the fish grill racks remembering to secure them with the clamps provided. Put the chop-loaded grill racks on bricks set up as in the illustration, or, if you have a set of brass andirons for your hearth, now's your chance to use them. Feel free to improvise. The main thing is to keep the lamb suspended over the coals by 6-12 inches or thereabouts.

If you're forsaking the romance and using a grill, don't bother with the fish racks and just lay the chops on your regular grill. If you're using charcoal briquets in your outdoor grill (don't use briquets indoors), add wood chips soaked in water for two hours to provide the cooking smoke.

Napkin art no. 724

While the chops cook, prepare a green salad. A side of Joel's Quick-Grilled Potatoes is also well-suited to this meal, and can be prepared over the same coals. Jonny thinks cooking these chops anywhere past medium-rare is a sin, so he suggests a cooking time of at least five minutes a side, but this depends on many factors (the chops, the size of your fireplace, the fire) so you'll just have to see for yourself.

When they're done, remove the chops from the fire, unclamp the grill, pour the wine and enjoy them in the soft glow of the fire's embers.

Quick Mesquite-Grilled Butterflied Leg of Lamb with Classic English Mint Sauce

Some years back Jonny was chef at Alberta's, a trendy, new mesquite-grill restaurant in the historic waterfront section of Portland known as the Old Port. On its first Saturday night the restaurant was so busy the roast leg of lamb sold out with a speed that no one, least of all Jonny, had counted on. In a panic, the restaurant's proprietor rushed off to the nearest market for another leg of lamb. Jonny butterflied and rubbed it, and then bunged it onto the mesquite wood grill in record time.

The waiters, apprehensive because their patrons had expected roast leg of lamb, sent Jonny out to explain. The dish was so well received it remains on the menu to this day, 10 years later. Jonny keeps a jar of the lamb rub he concocted that night at home should unexpected guests drop by.

There is enough lamb here to feed six hungry, soon to be appreciative, people.

- 1 5-6 pound leg of lamb, butterflied
- 3 Tablespoons Ram Island Lamb Rub
- 4 large cloves of garlic, peeled and sliced lengthwise
- 1/2 teaspoon kosher salt
- 1/2 teaspoon black pepper, freshly ground
- 3 Tablespoons melted margarine
- mesquite charcoal

☞ **For the sauce**
- 1/2 cup chopped fresh mint leaves (or 1/8 cup dry mint leaves)
- 1/8 cup HP malt, sherry or cider vinegar
- 1/8 cup granulated sugar
- 1 Tablespoon shallot, finely chopped
- 1/2 Tablespoon kosher salt
- 1 teaspoon black pepper, freshly ground
- 1/4 cup water

Your butcher will bone and trim your leg of lamb when you ask for it butterflied. Don't let him throw the bones away, you paid for them, bring them home and save them in the freezer for a St. Patty's Day Irish stew. The lamb Jonny uses is from Maine, but use whatever's available to you.

Crank up a medium-hot fire, using mesquite charcoal if you can get it. Kingsford's mesquite-laced briquets or regular briquets with water-soaked mesquite chips will serve as a good substitute. If you happen to be in a part of the country where grape vines or juniper cuttings are available, throw them in with the charcoal.

With a sharp knife cut small, deep slits into the fleshy side of the lamb and insert the garlic slivers, the more the merrier. Massage in the Ram Island Lamb Rub and the salt and pepper, then slather on the margarine.

Put the lamb on the grill, fleshy side down, over the hottest part of the fire to sear it. The coals will flare up but don't panic, that won't last. After a couple of minutes flip over the meat using long-handled tongs and let the other side sear for two minutes, just long enough to put those nice grill markings on it, like you see on TV.

After each side has been seared, move the lamb to a more indirect heat on the grill and close the cover, leaving the vents half-open. Cook about 45 minutes. The exact cooking time will depend upon how you like your lamb, but 45 minutes seems to satisfy most people. The internal temperature should be somewhere in the vicinity of 150°F. The lamb doesn't need to be turned or touched as it cooks, which leaves you plenty of time to mix the sauce.

To make the sauce, combine all ingredients in a jar with a tight-fitting lid, shake well and set aside. The sauce keeps for months when refrigerated.

Jonny prefers British malt vinegar in this sauce. HP malt vinegar is good and readily available. This sauce will convert people who think that the only accompaniment to lamb is mint jelly from the jar.

Remove the lamb from the grill and let it sit on a platter for 10 minutes, then slice thinly across the grain. Shake the sauce and pour a little over the top. Serve the rest on the side.

Try roasted potatoes or homemade shoestring French fries and a medley of fresh, grilled baby vegetables with this dish. A California cabernet sauvignon will wash it down nicely.

FISH & SEAFOOD

Grill-Kippered Salmon

•

Terriyaki Bluefish Barbeque and Cracklins

•

Grilled Lobster Two Lights

•

Jerk Lobster

•

Schyla Jean's Jewel Island Skillet Shrimp Feast

•

Brook Trout and Proscuitto in Foil

•

A Downeast Clam Bake for 125 Nice Folks

In a state where lobster appears almost everywhere, including the license plates of cars, seafood is not simply a commodity, it is a part of everyday Maine life. The first settlers came to these waters for whale oil, and not finding it, fished for all manner of seafood. Mussels were harvested from the islands, clam flats were staked out, rockweed was gathered for bakes and alderwood cut for the fire.

Hundreds of lobster, shrimp and scallop boats work Maine's coves, bays and off-shore banks. It's a hard business, as even the stoic Uncle Billy will admit. One cold, early morning on a lobster boat was all he needed to convince him to stick to trout fishing and smelt shacks. Now he's content to relieve fisherman of their shack fish at the pool hall next door, keeping his pool cue chalked and both feet firmly on dry land.

Much of what Maine takes from the sea leaves the state, and often, the country. Tuna, sea urchins and Maine shrimp are air-freighted to the Far East on a regular basis, while in the U.S. and Europe, the lobster people eat in Kansas City and Zurich is, most likely, a Maine lobster. Finding good, fresh seafood to buy in Maine is no tougher than finding a wheat field in Nebraska.

As Mister George Herbert Walker Bush down in Kennebunkport well knows, finding fish to catch can be an iffy sort of thing. The fish don't know it's the President's hook they're passing up, or that the local Portland newspaper has been keeping a front-page count on his string of fishless days. Nephew Jonny has considerably better luck, maybe because he doesn't have a press-loaded ferry doing donuts around the presidential fishing skiff, or maybe Jonny just knows the waters better. (If you can dodge the scribes, Mr. President, Jonny's got the cooler loaded.)

Between the lobsters (which are pricey one day and dirt cheap the next) and the bluefish, pogies and Maine shrimp (none of which ever cost much in the first place), there is always enough reasonably-priced seafood around to keep people at Uncle Billy's happy.

Whether it's lobster you buy, sea urchins you dive for, salmon or trout you catch on a dry fly, bluefish you troll for, or mussels you pry from the island rocks, no place has better tasting seafood than Maine. As Uncle Billy says, "That's not prejudice, that's fact."

Jonny stoking the rig at
"Memphis in May" BBQ competition.

Grill-Kippered Salmon

When Uncle Billy's mother cooked salmon and peas for supper she used either land-locked salmon from Sebago Lake, or Atlantic salmon caught by fishermen with great, long fly rods.

The business of fish farming has made procuring fresh salmon a significantly easier proposition than casting with long fly rods. Atlantic salmon, the kind Maine fish farmers raise, has a high-oil content, which makes it an ideal item for the barbeque grill. A barbequed fish is a kippered fish.

West Coast salmon, like king and coho, are also very flavorful when kippered, but they do not have as high a fat content as their Atlantic brethren, so you have to be more careful, lest it overcook and dry out. By the way, the fat we're talking about here is what nutritionists call omega-3 fatty acids. This kind of fat is good for you, and the more the better. Although we'd eat them anyway, it's nice to know that not everything tasty has a warning label attached to its underbelly.

In the warmer months, when Uncle Billy's Barbeque caters weddings and other celebrations, Jonny often prepares Grill-Kippered Salmon in barrel grills right behind the serving table.

Six ounces of kippered salmon makes a good entree portion. This recipe serves eight.

- 6-pound whole Atlantic salmon, filleted and scaled
- 1 Vidalia onion (1/4 pound), peeled and sliced into thin rounds
- 1 teaspoon kosher salt
- 1/2 teaspoon black peppercorns, fresh-cracked
- 1 Tablespoon olive oil
- 2 ounces fresh, whole dill sprigs
- 1 handful of soaked fruitwood chips, or alder if you can get it

Remove the feather bones from the salmon fillets. Better yet, get your fishmonger to do it for you.

Make a shallow, medium-low heat fire in your grill and let it burn 15-20 minutes. Add the chips. Place the fillets skin-side down on the grill. Sprinkle the salt and olive oil onto the flesh of the salmon. Then evenly distribute the onions and dill weed (stalks and all) on the fish. Cover the grill, almost completely closing the vents. If your grill does not have a cover, put a sheet of aluminum foil over the fish, using stones to anchor the foil. Remember, your fire should not be too hot, nothing more than a good bed of coals, no roaring blaze here.

HONING YOUR DEBONING

Run your finger tips along the fillets to locate the feather bones. Grasp the end of each bone with needle-nose pliers and pull them out, one by one. The process may sound tiresome, but after a few minutes it becomes second-nature and proceeds rapidly.

After 20-25 minutes the flesh of the salmon will turn a lighter shade of pink and should flake easily. It would be a shame to overcook this noble fish, so keep your large metal spatulas handy to remove it as soon as the salmon is done.

Remove the fillets to large, warm serving platters, being careful to keep them intact.

Jonny serves a homemade remoulade sauce as an accompaniment. It includes all the things that are good with fish, like capers, fresh parsley, dill and tarragon, Dijon mustard and real homemade mayonnaise. While remoulade recipes are available in many cookbooks, Jonny prefers using Blackburn's Remoulade Sauce, which he thinks is as good as any he could make.

Terriyaki Bluefish Barbeque and Cracklins

During the summer months, bluefish is one of the most reasonably priced saltwater fish on the market. They become so plentiful that lobstermen use them as bait. They are also great fun to catch, either at the beach or in a boat.

Two of Jonny's favorite catches are bluefish and Kennebec River striped bass. Once or twice a year, something makes the blues particularly vicious. On those days the blues run the mackerel and pogies right onto the beach. Then when the tide is out, Jonny'll go down to Kettle Cove, near his mother's house, and fill five-gallon pails with blues left behind in tidal pools, keeping a Louisville Slugger nearby in case one gets out of hand.

Bluefish are relative newcomers to local waters. Blame it on the ozone, global warming or the nuke plant up Wiscasset-way. Whatever the reason, Uncle Billy and Nephew Jonny are glad they can catch a few for the smoker.

When buying bluefish, make sure the fillets look and smell fresh, and the flesh has a good, firm texture. Cut away and discard the dark strips of meat. If you fillet the fish yourself, be careful of the sharp dorsal fin.

Bluefish shrink a bit during cooking. This recipe will feed four.

- 1 3-pound bluefish fillet
- 1 Tablespoon melted margarine
- 1 Tablespoon safflower oil
- 2 drops sesame oil
- 1/4 cup scallions, finely chopped
- 1 handful soaked alderwood or corn cob chips

☞ For the Marinade
- 1 ounce cooking sherry
- 1 ounce fresh ginger, peeled
- 1 large clove fresh garlic, peeled
- 2 Tablespoons soy sauce
- 2 Tablespoons brown sugar

☞ For the Dipping Sauce
- 2 Tablespoons soy sauce
- 1 Tablespoon prepared horseradish

To make the marinade, combine the sherry, peeled ginger and garlic in a food processor or blender and liquefy. Then add the soy sauce and brown sugar and blend thoroughly.

Place the bluefish fillet in a shallow baking or casserole dish and pour the marinade over the fish. Cover and refrigerate overnight, or for at least two hours.

Start the fire, get it medium-hot to hot and add the chips.

Brush both sides of the bluefish with the melted margarine, then sear the fillet on the grill flesh-side down, over the hottest part of the fire. If it curls up, make shallow incisions in the skin with a sharp knife. After a minute or two, carefully turn the fillet and sear the other side. It shouldn't stick.

With both sides seared move the fish to indirect heat, keeping the fish skin-side down. Cover and cook 35-40 minutes with the vents half-open. Check your fire for flare-ups occasionally.

While the fillet barbeques, prepare the dipping sauce. Stir the horseradish into the soy sauce and set aside.

When you remove the fillet using two large steel spatulas you will find that the skin has developed an affinity for the metal grill. That's normal. Remove the meat, place on a warmed serving platter and set aside in a warm oven.

Go back to the grill and remove the bluefish skin. It will probably break into several pieces. This is also fine because you're going to chop it in a minute anyway. Discard any overly-burnt parts, then put the skin on the cutting board and cut the crisp skin into small pieces.

Napkin art no. 311

In a skillet, heat the safflower and sesame oils until hot but not smoking. Add the strips of bluefish skin, moving them around now and then with a long-handled wooden spoon. Cook for a couple of minutes then drain the cracklins on a paper towel. Arrange the strips on the bluefish fillet, garnish with the chopped scallions and serve with the dipping sauce on the side.

Hypnotizing a Lobster

As a humane gesture toward the lobster before cooking — or just for the hell of it — here's how to hypnotize a lobster:

Basically, you're going to lull the lobster into crustacean bliss by giving it a Swedish massage of sorts. To do this, using two fingers, stroke along the back from head to tail a few times. The lobster will love it and become still. Now, grasp him near the fins at the end of his tail and lift all but the head and claws off the table, placing him in a headstand position. Spread his claws to out from his sides to act as ballast. A lobster hypnotized this way will remain dormant for 15 or 30 seconds. You can't ask them to sing or dance or do stupid pet tricks; except for one, but that's better saved for the Letterman show.

Should you want to cure yourself of the compassion to send lobsters on a pre-consumption bliss trip, try one of Uncle Billy's cures. The first is to work at a big lobster bake some hot, summer day. On or about your fiftieth lobster, any desire to hypnotize them will vanish. The other way is to buy a fiesty three pounder, place him on your kitchen counter, take the bands off of his claws and finger wrestle with him. After you heal, you'll never feel such compassion for them again.

Grilled Lobster Two Lights

Two Lights State Park, right outside of Portland, Maine, was named, with typical Yankee understatement, for the two lighthouses that sit side-by-side off the easternmost tip of Cape Elizabeth. It is also where Nephew Jonny grew up. When he named his favorite lobster dish, Jonny, relying on that same Yankee flair for words, came up with Grilled Lobster Two Lights, and he offers it here for your enjoyment.

This recipe serves two and is simplicity itself to double or triple.

- 2 1¼-pound hardshell lobsters
- 2 Tablespoons olive oil
- salt and fresh ground pepper

After you have hypnotized the lobster hold him down firmly by the tail, avoiding the claws, and with a large, very sharp chef's knife, insert the blade into the fissure approximately two inches behind the eyes, severing the spinal cord.

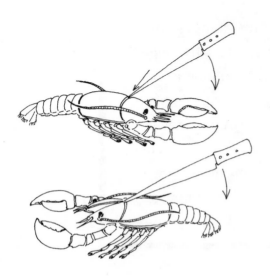

Then, with a paper-cutter motion, bring the blade down to the cutting board, splitting the lobster in half lengthwise. Turn the lobster 180 degrees and split the remainder in half again, using the same motion. Twist off the claws where they join the body, lay them on the cutting board and whap them with the blunt side of the knife. The object is to crack them, not hit them so hard that there's lobster parts all over the place.

Rub the claws and their knuckles with olive oil, wrap loosely in aluminum foil and place them on the hot part of a medium-hot charcoal fire. Cover and close the vents halfway. These parts take longer than the rest of the lobster, so don't wait to get them cooking.

Remove the stomach from the body of the lobster; it's right behind the eyes (which may, or may not, say a lot about the psychology of *Homarus americanus*, which is uptown for lobster). You'll also see a blue vein running through the tail, take that out. Leave in the tomally (green stuff), if you like. The same goes for the rest of whatever else is in there; who knows, it might even be good for you.

Brush or rub the remaining lobster meat with olive oil, rubbing whatever oil is left onto the shell. Sprinkle with salt and pepper and place, shell-side down, right over the coals. Cover, leaving the vents half-shut. Leave the claws and knuckles on the grill next to the lobster. It'll all be finished in 20 minutes or so.

Remove from the grill, and serve. While those funny looking bibs are optional, corn on the cob and smoked red potatoes and Green Tomato ChowChow ought to be required accompaniments.

To make a truly distinctive butter sauce for dipping the lobster meat, add a half-teaspoon (or a touch more) of jerk sauce to a stick of melted butter, squeeze in the juice of half a lemon, stir and serve in a small bowl, crock or ramekin. Jonny sometimes looks up Julia Childs' Bernaise sauce recipe and has it with his Grilled Lobster Two Lights. Any way you do it, it won't be wrong.

Jerk Lobster

Soon after Nephew Jonny began making and bottling the elixir, Voodoo Jerk Slather Sauce, there was a time when almost anything edible got slathered. This explains why there's so much jerk on the menu: jerk chicken, jerk chicken wings, jerk pogie and menhaden, jerk spaghetti and other savory concoctions. The regulars who frequent the place love their jerk every which way.

One day a friend of Jonny's picked up a couple of three-pounders down on the waterfront before stopping in at Uncle Billy's, which was on his way home. As luck would have it, he stopped by during one of Jonny's early jerk frenzies and wound up trading his lobsters for a rack of pork ribs and a quart of Barbeque Billy Beans. Jonny had one of the barrel grills stoked up and a bottle of jerk sauce handy, the result was nothing short of spectacular.

Even Uncle Billy, who has been off lobster since his time out lobstering some 30 years back, gives this preparation his unqualified endorsement, "Only damn way to eat them sea bugs."

- 2 1¼-pound hardshell lobsters (one per person)

☞ **For each lobster**
- 1 Tablespoon olive oil
- 1/2 Tablespoon Jerk Slather sauce
- pinch salt
- pinch fresh ground black pepper

Hypnotize the lobster just as you did for Grilled Lobster Two Lights. In fact, turn back to that recipe and follow the preparation directions up to, and including, the part about rubbing the claws and knuckles with olive oil. Then come back to this page and slather some jerk sauce into the cracks in the shell.

Place the foil-wrapped claws directly over the coals of a medium-hot grill and cover, leaving the vents half-open. Since these appendages take longer to cook than the rest of the lobster, start them 10 minutes before you add the rest.

Remove the stomach from the lobster, the blue vein from the tail, and, depending upon your likes or dislikes, that green liver googa, which is called tomally by the people who eat it and googa by those of us who don't.

Rub the remaining olive oil onto the meat of the lobster tail, using whatever is left over to rub on the shell. Sprinkle with salt and pepper, then rub in the jerk sauce, wearing rubber kitchen gloves.

Place the lobster body and tail shell-side down on the grill, next to the claws and put back the cover. Everything will be finished in 20 minutes. Remove from the grill, unwrap the foil and they're ready to eat.

Serve with potatoes, Damned Good Sweet Onions and corn that you've cooked on the grill. If you're feeling extra brave, serve them with the jerk butter slather from Grilled Lobster Two Lights. Add a bottle or two of a nice, oakey, cold California Chardonnay, Geary's ale or a pitcher of ice-cold lemonade. You'll need them.

Schyla Jean's Jewel Island Skillet Shrimp Feast

Come winter, Maine shrimp begin to show up on the docks and on the roadsides; sold off the back of pickup trucks up and down Coastal Route One. They're only available for a few months, and Jonny's wife takes this opportunity to make what he fondly calls Schyla Jean's Jewel Island Skillet Shrimp Feast. It's a nice treat for him on his day off and since the kids love it too, Schyla gets more than a few requests for this dish. So despite the fact that this is not, strictly speaking, a barbeque recipe, it is here nonetheless, for your enjoyment.

If you don't happen to be in Maine in the winter, you can substitute the small gulf shrimp known as U-30's (which means about 30 shrimp to the pound) that come frozen, with the head off but the shell on. Crawfish tails are also a worthy substitute.

This recipe feeds Jonny and Schyla and the two smaller kids, but doubling it is easy. Just bring out another skillet and some more newspaper.

Jewel Island is the outermost island in Casco Bay, Schyla Jean's favorite spot for summer sailboat picnics. It's also the one the shrimp boats pass on their way out to sea. And if that weren't enough, it's also where Captain Kidd is rumored to have buried his treasure; a treasure that Jonny has yet to find.

- 3 pounds Maine shrimp, head off/shell on
- 1/4 cup barbeque sauce
- 3 Tablespoons Black Pan Fish Mix
- 2 Tablespoons melted butter

In a large bowl, toss the shrimp with the Black Pan Fish Mix until they are thoroughly coated. Pour in the melted butter and toss them again. Get a heavy iron frying pan very hot and put in the shrimp. If you're cooking indoors, turn your vent fan on High since there will be a fair bit of smoke. Schyla Jean makes this over a gas ring set up on the back porch, but if you don't have this arrangement, go ahead and cook them inside. The Black Pan Fish Mix can be a little pungent, so be careful not to inhale deeply during the first moments of cooking.

Stir the shrimp with a steel spatula, flipping them over now and then. Stir and flip for five minutes, over high heat. Then add the barbeque sauce, stir one last time, and put the skillet on a table that has been covered with layers of last Sunday's newspaper.

To eat, roll up your sleeves, suck the outside of the shrimp, then peel and eat. True, it's messy as all get-out, but you won't mind one bit after you've tasted the first one.

Jonny with two of the boys, Jourdan and Julian.
The oldest, Seth Bullmoose, is hiding.

Brook Trout and Proscuitto in Foil

We use brook trout, also known as brookies, in this preparation but smallmouth bass or any other variety of freshwater pan fish, including small salmon, work just as well.

Jonny first ate a sauteed trout preparation similar to this, in Portugal. He liked it so much that he adapted it to Uncle Billy cookery. It's important that the fish be fresh, thus the streamside preparation. If you don't catch any fish, the proscuitto will hold you until you get to the nearest rib joint.

- 2 whole brook trout, cleaned
- 1/4 teaspoon salt
- 1/2 teaspoon pepper
- 1 teaspoon olive oil
- 4 slices proscuitto ham, thinly sliced

Rinse the eviscerated trout in cold water and pat dry. Sprinkle the salt and pepper into the cavity. Cut a small fir bough with the saw blade of your Swiss Army Knife. Place the fir greens into the fish as well, and set the cuttings aside. Wrap each fish in two pieces of proscuitto, rub on the olive oil and wrap loosely in foil.

Set a small hibachi by the side of the stream, burn a wood fire down to coals, throw on the fir cuttings and place the foil-wrapped fish on the grill. Five minutes later you'll be digging into the best streamside meal you ever tasted.

A Downeast Clam Bake for 125 Nice Folks

Here in Maine, nothing touches the primordial nerve like a clam bake — the original American barbeque. A clam bake is barbeque at its most basic. The aromas of rockweed and wood smoke, and the briny smell of steaming shellfish, arouse the senses. A clam bake is a community event, be it a neighborhood, a reunion of old friends or a group of total strangers. Even Uncle Billy is moved to waxing sentimental about the Gulf of Maine when a clam bake is in full swing. He may not go out lobstering, dig for clams or harvest mussels and rockweed, but he's first in line when it's all served up, and first in line again for extra helpings.

Like barbeque sauces, the ingredients of a clam bake can get people's danders up right quick. Once upon a time Uncle Billy could fill the back of his pickup truck with bushel after bushel of clams and not even make a dent in the roll of cash he keeps on hand for pool playing and a little genteel carousing. These days the price of clams, even in Maine, has increased dramatically, forcing Billy to choose between carousing and clams. Clams lost. Considering the expense, Jonny and Uncle Billy have come to the conclusion that mixing in bushels of mussels is an awfully good idea. Economics aside, mussels are exceptionally good eating. You might find your guests actually prefer them.

Lobsters are, according to clam-bake purists, not a traditional clam bake item either. Nor is the use of eggs. Jonny aims for good eating, not historic preservation, and it's his considered opinion that lobster, clams and mussels, corn, potatoes, onions, sausage, eggs and chicken leaves everyone full and happy when the event is over and done.

A lot a lot of work goes into preparing a clam bake, so you might as well do it up big.

When Uncle Billy's Barbeque puts on a clambake everything comes to the feast as fresh as it can be had. Corn is picked that day, and the seafood comes from the docks that morning. The eggs are farm-fresh, as are the onions and potatoes. Depending upon your locale it may not be possible to get everything fresh-picked, just get as reasonably close as you can — that's all anyone can expect.

Many people in Maine, Jonny among them, keep a hoe, a hod and fisherman's rubber gloves in the back of his truck, along with an empty bushel basket or two, a fishing pole and some unidentifiable rubber tubing that he claims came with the vehicle. The hoe is technically known as a clam rake, but nobody round here calls them that, they just call them a hoe because that's what they are.

To get the rockweed and mussels, Jonny takes a small boat out to one of the islands that dot the coast of Maine. When he's out there he fills empty onion sacks with rockweed, and other sacks with mussels.

Jonny's got the necessary papers and permits and likes harvesting his ingredients, but you don't have to. Like salmon, farm-grown mussels are available worldwide, as are Maine lobsters. Clams are local to most coastal states and just about everyone knows where to pick up fresh ears of corn, onions, potatoes, eggs and chicken.

$\mathbf{T}$here are a number of ways to construct the apparatus for the bake. Jonny suggests that you get two 4 x 5-foot sheets of steel at least 1/8-inch thick; 1/4-inch is better but heavy to tote. He sets them up on concrete blocks and covers the whole thing with a canvas tarp.

☞ **Materials for the Cooker**
- 2, 4 x 5-foot sheets of steel, 1/8 inch thick
- 7 large cinder blocks
- 1, 6 x 12-foot (approx.) canvas tarp or tent

☞ **For the Fire**
- 50 pounds dry hardwood, or alder
- 1 bushel dry kindling

$\mathbf{H}$ave some strong friends hold the steel sheets a few feet off the ground while you position the cinder blocks at the corner of each sheet, and one block at the middle spot. The two sheets should overlap by a foot.

- 5 bushels rockweed or seaweed
- 3 bushels clams
- 3 bushels fresh sweet corn
- 125 1¼-pound lobsters
- 2 bushels mussels
- 1 bushel new potatoes
- 1 bushel small, new onions
- 30 broiler chickens, quartered
- 30 pounds homemade sausage (or kielbasa), in coils
- 12 dozen eggs
- 8 pounds unsalted butter
- 4 dozen lemons, quartered
- 2 squirt jars Visine

Distribute the wood and kindling evenly beneath where the steel sheets will go, and start the fire. Get it going very hot and then quickly place the steel into position. Soak two bushels of rockweed with buckets of fresh or salt water, then dump one bushel of the rockweed in the center of each sheet and loosely spread it around with a rake.

Put the mussels and clams into loosely-tied stockinette bags, 7 or 8 pounds to the bag. Put the eggs, onions and potatoes in these bags as well, about a dozen to the bag. The bags are available from catering and cooking supply stores (panty hose will do in a pinch).

If it's at all possible, first partially cook the chickens and the sausage in a 350°F degree oven or barbeque rig for 25-30 minutes. Otherwise, with the rockweed steaming and the fire raging, bung on the chicken quarters and sausage coils (wrapped loosely in foil) 25 minutes before everything else. Layer the chicken and sausage on top of the first rockweed layer, cover with a second layer and place the thoroughly wetted canvas over the whole lot. Once in place, lightly hose down the canvas, being careful not to douse the fire.

Hose down the corn while still in crates. After the chicken and sausage have been on the fire 25 minutes remove the tarp and distribute the ears on the hot rockweed. Add the onions and potatoes. Then add lobsters to this layer and then cover with a bunch more wet rockweed. If you pre-cooked the chicken and sausage, place them on the fire now with the corn and lobster.

Next, position the bags of mussels and eggs around the outside where you can keep an eye on them.

Cover the steaming pile with the remaining, well-dampened rockweed. Thoroughly wet the canvas tarp and again use it to cover the whole bake. The tarp should be large enough to tuck under the edges of the steel sheets by a few inches. Keep an eye on the tarp, you may need to wet it down again. These tarps seem to want to ignite around the edges, where they meet the steel.

One of the more entertaining sights at a clam bake is watching the cook and his helpers run around the pit to avoid the smoke and swirling winds. This is where the Visine comes in.

After 45 minutes lift up an edge of the tarp, open a bag of eggs and take one out. If the egg is hard-boiled, the clam bake is ready.

While some helpers remove the tarp and others bring the side dishes to the serving tables, melt eight pounds of butter and pour half into a couple of #10- or quart-sized cans. Pull back the husks and dip the corn into the butter, and serve. This is hot stuff, so bring along your heavy rubber gloves. Put the remaining butter into metal bowls, for the lobster, and set on each table. If you like, mix some lemon juice and Voodoo Jerk Slather Sauce into some of the melted butter, and stir. Set plates of the quartered lemons on the table. Besides squeezing the lemons on the lobster, clams and mussels, the juice is good for cleaning your hands after the feed.

Traditionally a clam broth is served on the side for dipping. You can make it by holding back a peck or two of clams or mussels. As the rest of the food cooks, boil them in a large pot with a couple of inches of water and a few bay leaves. When everything is ready, strain this broth into metal bowls and put them on the tables alongside the clams.

Serve buffet style. Every plate should have a lobster, ear of corn, clams and mussels, a piece of sausage and chicken, an egg, some onions, potatoes, butter and clam broth. Set your company down on a piece of sandy beach and watch them sup in appreciative silence — save for the cracking of shells, of course.

WILD GAME

Over The Line Wild Boar Ribs

•

Hannaford Cove Hearth-Roast Pheasant

•

Merrymeeting Bay Mud-Baked Duck

•

Grilled Venison Chops with Juniper and Gin

We hardly see game in Portland anymore, but not too long ago a moose went for a swim in Back Cove, a body of water bounded on three sides by parks, houses and a University, and on the fourth by an interstate highway bridge near the B & M Baked Bean factory. With the help of the harbor patrol, a lobster boat and two game wardens, the moose came ashore, was sedated and driven a few miles out of town, to an area better suited to quiet, near-sighted mammals.

In recent years Uncle Billy has taken to fishing more than hunting, but Jonny still heads out when he has a chance, using a bow for venison and an old side-by-side 12-gauge for birds and water fowl. The chance to get outdoors draws him as much as the fresh game. Even if Jonny's unlucky in the hunt, he usually has an adequate supply of venison on hand thanks to the friends who bring him deer to butcher.

If you live in a part of the country that deer seldom visit and ducks don't land in the hot tub, take heart — you can special order venison or boar ribs from your butcher or by telephone. Don't miss out on the outdoors part, though. While the meat marinates, take the kids and the dog and go for a walk in the woods or nearby park. Then go home and fire up the grill.

Over The Line Wild Boar Ribs

Boar is not indigenous to New England. They were introduced to the upper Connecticut River Valley in the 1800s by a wealthy Bavarian immigrant, a nobleman by some accounts, who brought the animals in for his own sport. They bred with runaway domestic pigs, and the result is a breed of wild boar that still roam the northern reaches of the Connecticut River Valley.

A few years back Uncle Billy and Nephew Jonny set off on a wild boar hunting expedition. They went over the line into New Hampshire's White Mountains, equipped with what Uncle Billy called, "Enough armaments to bring down a fair-sized tractor at a hundred yards."

They returned empty-handed, though their wits were severely rattled by a couple of, in Uncle Billy's words, "Damned unfriendly looking hogs — and big? B'jesus but they were some wicked fierce-looking." Jonny talks about tusks a half-mile long, but even Uncle Billy laughs at that part. People who have actually seen a wild boar, however, don't tease Jonny about his elongated memory of charging boar tusks. You see, the bayonet was invented in Germany as a sporting tool intended to keep the wounded boar at bay.

Should your life insurance representative persuade you that Disneyworld would make a better vacation than a boar hunt, take heart; boar ribs are available from specialty butchers and many gourmet shops. The boar will likely be a smaller animal, and quite probably from Texas while the boar ribs from northern New England are closer to the classic boar of Bavaria. As with any farm-raised versus wild-caught meat, wild game is more intense in flavor. Just follow the recipe and you will be pleased with the results, even if you don't get to be scared half out of your wits by a charging boar.

This recipe will feed six people.

- 6 1/2-pound racks of boar rib

☞ **For the Marinade**
- 1 cup dry red wine
- 1/4 cup dry sherry
- 1/4 cup cognac
- 1 small onion, thinly sliced
- 1 carrot, thinly sliced
- 2 Tablespoons fresh parsley leaves, coarsely chopped
- 1 Tablespoon shallots, coarsely chopped
- 1 Tablespoon olive oil
- 2 teaspoons fresh black peppercorns
- 1 teaspoon kosher salt
- 1 teaspoon granulated garlic
- 1 teaspoon dried thyme leaves
- 1/2 teaspoon allspice
- 6 bay leaves
- 1/8 cup Barbados molasses
- 4 ounces beer
- 1 handful soaked hardwood or corn cob chips

Mix together all the marinade ingredients (except the molasses and beer) and pour into large, shallow, rectangular metal baking or roasting pans. Add the ribs, cover with plastic wrap and put in the refrigerator overnight. Every now and again turn the ribs in the pans to thoroughly soak each side. You can soak the chips now too, or if you prefer, wet them a couple of hours before starting the fire.

The next day, build a medium-hot fire. Throw on the chips and set the ribs over an indirect heat; cover, leaving the vents half-open. Go inside, open a can of beer, pour 3/4 of it into your glass and the remainder into a pot with the leftover marinade. Stir in the molasses and bring to a boil on the stove, stirring well. Reduce the heat, simmer and continue to stir. After 10 minutes take the marinade, which is now a baste, outside and slather it on the ribs.

Napkin art no. 910

Cover the grill, leaving the vents half-open and cook for 60-90 minutes, basting until the marinade is gone.

Serve racks whole, arming each guest with a steak knife. If the knives don't easily cut their way through the ribs, bung the racks back on the grill — you're not cooking souffle here. Put some No Bean Shotgun Succotash and maybe a jar of applesauce on the table and ring the chow bell.

Hannaford Cove Hearth-Roast Pheasant

In the planted-over winter fields near Uncle Billy's house in Cape Elizabeth, pheasant are abundant. In fact, it was near his uncle's house that Jonny first hunted. His first dinner trophy was pheasant.

Because of the low percentage of fat in pheasant, this recipe works well in your living room fireplace, provided you use some common sense, like not setting hot coals on the Oriental rug you inherited from your great-aunt.

This makes a nice dinner for four.

- 2, 1-1½ pound pheasants
- 1/4 pound melted margarine
- 2 ounces Worcestershire sauce
- 2 Tablespoons lemon juice
- 1 Tablespoon Hungarian paprika
- 1/2 teaspoon black pepper, freshly ground
- 1/2 teaspoon kosher salt

After the pheasants have been plucked and cleaned, split them in half (removing and discarding the breast bone). Wash thoroughly in cold water and pat dry. In a small bowl combine the Worcestershire sauce, lemon juice, paprika, salt and pepper to make a baste. Stir well and brush this mixture into each side of the birds, then slather on the melted margarine. About one-third of the baste should be reserved for use on the birds as they cook.

Start a fire in your fireplace, using hardwood, such as red oak or maple. Keep the pheasants in the refrigerator until your fire has burned almost to embers. Set up some bricks to make a small stand for your grill to sit on, in a spot where there will be a medium heat when the fire dies down. If you have a Tuscan brazier grill, here's a good place to use it.

Clamp the birds into your fish grill. Sear both sides for 60 seconds, three inches or so from the coals. Now add a few more bricks to raise your grill stand to 12 inches above the coals. Cook skin-side up for 25-30 minutes brushing them with leftover marinade.

Place half a bird on each plate and serve with a side of Coal Roasted Sweet Potatoes and fiddleheads. A red wine, perhaps a California Merlot or a pinot noir from Washington State, would be appropriate.

*Grandmother Alice and Jonny
on his first birthday.*

Merrymeeting Bay Mud-Baked Duck

In 1775, Jonny's great-great-great-great grandfather, Ben Arnold, on his mother's side of the family, marched an army through Maine (which was a part of the Massachusetts colony back then) up the Kennebec River to the Chaudiere River in an attempt to take Quebec from the British. General Arnold, on orders from George Washington himself, met up with General Montgomery and his army, and together they marched on Quebec. Sir Guy Charleton, Great Britain's commanding officer, however, kicked their collective butts.

Jonny spends a lot of time on the Kennebec, the same river great-granddaddy Arnold marched along, in an area known as Merrymeeting Bay. Merrymeeting Bay has long been known for its good hunting and wild rice. The rice is not commercially harvested and attracts a variety of birds and ducks to the bay.

In the winter Jonny sets up a smelt shack for smelting; come spring he's fishing for striped bass, and in the autumn it's Merrymeeting Bay Duck he's after. He sometimes drags Uncle Billy with him who, once he gets through bellyaching about the cold or the heat, or the pitching of the boat, makes good company.

The mud on the banks of the bay is a potter's-quality clay. Jonny uses the mud for baking the duck and keeping the kids happily occupied. You can use store-bought potter's clay to achieve the same results.

This recipe serves four if the ducks are big enough. As far as substitutes go, a domestic farm-raised duck will do fine if your trigger finger is rusty or you get hungry for this meal outside duck season. A goose makes a fine substitute.

- 2 wild ducks, any kind
- 1 ounce fresh ginger, peeled
- 1 ounce cooking sherry
- 1 Tablespoon Five Spice Powder
- 1/2 teaspoon granulated garlic
- 1/2 teaspoon kosher salt
- 4 lotus leaves, or banana leaves
- 1/2 teaspoon sesame oil
- 1/8 cup Hoisin sauce
- 4 apples, peeled and quartered
- 3 Spanish onions (medium-small), peeled
- 2-3 pounds of clay

Puree the peeled ginger with the sherry in a food processor or blender. Rinse the cleaned and plucked ducks thoroughly with cold water and pat dry. Rub the inside and outside of the ducks with Five Spice Powder, salt, granulated garlic and the ginger-sherry puree. Wrap the ducks in plastic wrap and refrigerate overnight. Also, rehydrate the lotus or banana leaves in the fridge overnight as well.

You'll find lotus leaves at most Oriental markets. Banana leaves are available frozen at Oriental and Hispanic markets, and sometimes fresh at florist shops. If you're using frozen banana leaves, defrost them for a few minutes and they're ready to use. Get enough leaves to completely wrap the birds.

The next day, mix together the sesame oil and Hoisin sauce and slather it onto the birds, working liberal amounts of the mixture into and under the skin.

Stuff the quartered apples and the whole onions into the birds' cavities. (The apples will absorb the grease and be discarded, the onions are for eating.) Prick the breasts and thighs of the ducks with a fork and then start the fire.

You'll need plenty of charcoal to surround the birds, so pile about five pounds in your grill and build a hot fire.

Back inside, wrap the birds in the leaves, tying the bundle with string or butcher's twine. Moisten the clay with water and then use a rolling pin to flatten the clay into a half-inch thick circular shape that's wide enough to wrap around each duck. Sprinkle water onto the clay as needed to keep it pliable. If you're cooking more than one duck, divide the clay. Set each duck in the middle of its piece of clay and work the clay so that it completely envelops the duck. Use water as you go to blend seams and repair cracks.

By this time your charcoal fire ought to be a mess of white hot coals about six-inches deep.

Using a fireplace shovel or large metal spoon with a very long handle, bury the clay-covered birds in the coals, seam side up. Cover the clay with the coals as much as possible. Almost completely close your grill vents and let the birds cook for 2½ hours.

Wild rice goes nicely with this dish, so prepare your favorite dish while the ducks bake.

When the birds are done, using your fireplace shovel, remove the clay pots onto a non-ceramic platter — pewter is perfect. Gather your guests around for the show, and using a hefty hammer, ceremoniously crack open the clay and unwrap the leaves. Remove and slice the onions, discard the apples, and serve with appropriate fanfare.

If your guests don't applaud this effort, leave the Death By Chocolate Souffle in the refrigerator until after they leave.

*Billy (right) at 7, dressed sharp
for his First Communion, and
Jonny at 3, Christmas Day.*

Grilled Venison Chops with Juniper and Gin

Uncle Billy used to go deer hunting, Jonny still does now and again, but never in early November at season's opening when the woods are full of half-crazed and heavily-armed flatlanders from points south. That's the time of year Jonny dresses in orange-colored clothing and keeps the dog, the kids and cat well away from the woods.

If you don't hunt, there are, as we see it, three ways to obtain venison. Your friendly market or corner butcher can special order venison for you. Most likely the venison you will receive is from a New Zealand Red Deer, a slightly larger cousin to the New England White Tail. Many of the farms raising these Red Deer are right here in Maine. Another option is to become the Archbishop of Canterbury. This gentleman receives a haunch of venison each year at Christmas, courtesy of the Queen's huntsmen. The third option is to rub down your pickup bumper with buck lure.

This recipe serves two.

- 4, 8-ounce double-cut venison loin chops
- 1 ounce gin
- 1 Tablespoon cracked black peppercorns
- 10 cracked juniper berries
- 1 teaspoon olive oil
- 1/2 teaspoon kosher salt
- 1 handful water-soaked applewood chips

Grind (crack) the peppercorns and juniper berries in a mortar and pestle. If you don't have a mortar and pestle, put the berries and peppercorns on a cutting board, lay the flat edge of a large chef's knife on top and press down with the palm of your hand to crush them.

Work the cracked juniper berries and peppercorns into the sides of the chops, followed by the salt, and brush on the olive oil.

When building the fire, remember that apples are one of a deer's preferred meals, which is why orchard owners don't think deer are cute. Jonny suggests sprinkling some applewood chips over a hot to medium-hot charcoal fire before adding the chops.

Grill each side of the chops for six minutes, which results in a medium-rare chop.

Remove the chops to a serving platter. Pour the gin into a small saucepan, warm it and carefully ignite with a

Napkin art no. 56

match. Pour it, flaming, over the chops. Uncle Billy likes to pour the gin over the chops before he lights it, but Jonny insists the first way is better. For maximum effect, the chops should arrive at the table while still flaming.

Barbeque in a Bowl

Real Acadian Jambalaya
•
A Gallon of Ranger Mel's Chili
•
Grandmother Alice's Red Flannel Hash
•
Potlatch Gumbo
•
Red Beans and Rice
•
Jonny's Downeast Fish Chowder
•
Sleepout Jonny's Barbeque Spaghetti

Downeast barbeque, by nature and necessity, is frugal cuisine. There's nothing more Yankee, or Franco-American, for that matter than being thrifty, and making whole new dinners out of leftovers (les restes) comes naturally to Mainers.

Grandmother Alice was a master at feeding large families. Her ability to stretch last night's dinner into tomorrow's night's supper is an inspiration to us time and again.

Some foods make better leftovers than others because their flavors marry well. The basic idea behind barbeque is a blending of natural meat, fish and poultry flavors with spices and smoke. The longer these flavors marry, the better they blend. Barbeque in a Bowl takes this concept a step further by adding new flavors via sauces, seasonings and stock from boiled down barbequed bones, and introducing rice, beans, spaghetti, potatoes and such to the mix.

The Ranger Mel MK-2
"Remember the Alamo" mobile cooker.

Real Acadian Jambalaya

Here's where the cajun influence swims into the St. Laurent family gene pool. About 300 years ago, when Nephew Jonny's ancestral relations were not yet ancestral, and were living north of Maine in French Acadie (now called Nova Scotia), the British decided to evict everyone and claim the land for themselves. The Acadians were rounded up and shipped to Spanish settlements in the Louisiana Territories.

Those Acadians who managed to elude capture made themselves scarce by heading to the hills. Among them were a number of St. Laurents. The British, determined to annex the territory, forced the remaining Acadians to disperse throughout Canada and, eventually into the mill towns of New England.

Over the years, the remnants of the family found each other. Through their letters and visits the cultures of north and south blended — one man's crawfish being another man's lobster — resulting in a culture richer than the original. Lest we forget, the source of the word *Cajun* is *Acadian*; and the jambalaya is superb.

You can ignore or freely substitute items on the ingredients list. Jonny always has a fair amount of pork around, so he puts plenty in his jambalaya. If, on the other hand, you have some barbequed turkey, a few sausage links, or a barbequed chicken or two lying about, they'll do just as well. Remember to save any bones to make the stock.

The stock will taste even better if you make it up the night before. If you don't have many bones around, a smoked ham hock makes a good substitute.

This recipe will feed a half-dozen folks easily, more if they're not St. Laurents.

- 1 stick margarine
- 1 pound Spanish onions, finely diced
- 4 small green bell peppers, finely diced
- 4 stalks celery, finely diced
- 2 heaping Tablespoons hot Hungarian paprika
- 1/2 pound diced Maine lobster, or crab meat
- 1/2 pound shrimp (If you're in Maine get Maine shrimp, if you're on the gulf get Gulf shrimp, if you're in the northwest get local pink shrimp, if you're in the midwest-get whatever you can, even crawfish.)
- 1 teaspoon salt
- 1/4 cup dried thyme leaves
- 1/4 cup fresh parsley, finely chopped
- 2 Tablespoons black pepper
- 1 Tablespoon white pepper
- 1 Tablespoon dry sage
- 1 heaping teaspoon cayenne pepper
- 6 bay leaves
- 2 pinches ground nutmeg
- 1 pound rough-chopped barbequed meat (pork, beef, poultry and link sausage)
- 1 pound white Carolina rice, uncooked
- 14-ounce can stewed tomatoes, diced, in their juice
- 14-ounce can tomato sauce
- 1 quart stock

☞ Stock
- 1½ quarts water
- pork and beef bones, poultry carcasses or a large ham hock

☞ Condiments
- 1 heaping Tablespoon file gumbo
- Tabasco or Voodoo Jerk Slather Sauce

For the stock: After pulling the meat from the bones and setting aside for later, put the bones and carcasses, and/or smoked ham hock, in a large stock pot.

For a quart of stock start with 1½ quarts of water in the pot. If you have any old carrots around, or some onion skins, toss them in. Simmer for two hours, adding water as needed to maintain at least a quart of liquid.

For the jambalaya: If the stock sat overnight in the refrigerator, remove the fat congealed around the top and then reheat. While the stock is reheating, prepare the other ingredients.

Melt half the margarine in a large skillet or saucepan and saute the vegetables over a medium heat, adding the paprika as they cook. After five minutes add the shellfish, salt and remaining spices (except for the file gumbo). Stir, add the meats, the rice, and the rest of the margarine, and keep stirring, using the spoon to make sure the rice gets thoroughly coated.

At this point add the tomatoes and their juice, the tomato sauce and the stock, which should now be at a boil. Cover the pot with foil, or a tight-fitting lid, and bring the jambalaya to a gentle boil. Remove from the stove and put into a pre-heated 350°F oven for 40 minutes.

When you remove the pot from the oven set it right on the table. Remove the cover and fluff up the mixture with a long carving fork, bringing what's on the bottom to the top. Spoon heaping portions into bowls and set them on the table. Sprinkle file gumbo atop each serving. Experiment with your favorite hot sauces. Uncle Billy shakes Voodoo Jerk Slather Sauce on his. Serve with cool beverages and a plate of fresh buttermilk biscuits or crusty French bread.

A Gallon of Ranger Mel's Chili

Chili and barbeque cook-offs are a big thing across the country, and in a particularly big way, down in the Lone Star State. During these events, vast quantities of chili and beer are consumed with gusto. In fact, it was at one of these Texas cook-offs that Uncle Billy ran into — quite literally, since he was well into the beer drinking part of the event at that moment — Ranger Mel. As will happen when two kindred, and slightly inebriated souls meet, all manner of things were discussed, among them some of the finer points of cooking beef brisket and making chili. Despite the circumstances under which these secrets were exchanged, Uncle Billy managed to return to Maine with some of them intact.

Today, Uncle Billy has Nephew Jonny make up batches of Ranger Mel's Chili. Most of the time he uses leftover beef brisket, just like Mel does. Or, if there is some handy, he'll use barbequed moose or venison. When Ranger Mel stops in, as he does from time to time on his way from Texas to Rockport, the three of them ladle out big bowls, open a case of beer, and start telling tall stories and outright lies.

Somewhere between the stories and the lies, there's always the debate about putting beans in chili. Mel doesn't; Billy does. Neither will give an inch one way or another, and Jonny has sense enough to stay out of the discussion altogether. In his recipe, though, Jonny, being a good New Englander, adds beans. Mel always asks for more, so it can't offend him too much, and Billy, by the end of the chili and the last of the beer, doesn't much care to argue.

Jonny's recipe feeds a whole lot of folks. Just how many depends on the folks themselves, but since it takes so long to cook, there's no sense in making just a little. Jonny emphasizes that the more burnt, marbled, charred, hacked-up, whooped-out and down-right nasty looking the leftover brisket, the better. While other cuts of meat, like London broil or chuck steak, will also work, both Ranger Mel and Uncle Billy prefer brisket.

As Billy is fond of saying, "There just ain't nothin' like it, so use it, and don't argue." And Billy's not lying.

- 2 pounds dried red kidney beans
- 3 quarts water
- 2 pounds leftover brisket, or other barbequed beef
- 1/8 cup vegetable oil
- 3 good-size green bell peppers, seeded and rough chopped
- 1 large head of garlic, peeled (or 6 heaping Tablespoons granu-
    lated garlic)
- 1 pound onion, any kind, rough chopped
- 6 heaping Tablespoons Hungarian paprika
- 4 heaping Tablespoons ground cumin
- 2 heaping Tablespoons coriander
- 1 heaping Tablespoon ground black pepper
- 1 level teaspoon cayenne pepper
- 1/2 teaspoon cloves
- 6 dried bay leaves
- 1/4 cup dried oregano
- 1/4 cup Masa tortilla flour (or regular cornmeal)
- 1 3-ounce package dried ancho or poblamo chilies, rehydrated
    and ground per instructions on package
- 3 fresh jalapeno peppers, finely chopped
- 3 cups red wine, cheap
- 2 cups coffee, day-old
- 1/8 cup soy sauce
- 1/8 cup Oriental fish sauce, or Worcestershire sauce
- 2 16-ounce cans stewed tomatoes, in juice
- 2 long-neck bottles Lone Star beer (or Guinness Stout)
- 1/8 cup molasses
- 2 ounces unsweetened chocolate

The beans will take longest to cook, so get started on them first. But first, wash and pick through them to make sure there aren't any stones, gravel or whatnot. Uncle Billy attributes the loss of a couple of his teeth to leaving out this step. Bring three quarts of water and the beans to an enthusiastic boil in an uncovered pot, then cover, take off the heat, and set aside for two hours — three's better.

In the meantime, hack the brisket into pieces about the size of your thumb. (If you're cooking the brisket just to make the chili and are not using leftovers, turn back to Brisket and Burnt Ends on page 68 for cooking instructions.) Put the oil into a large, heavy metal (but not stainless steel) pot, and heat the oil until almost smoking. Toss in the hacked-up brisket, bell peppers, garlic, onions and dry spices, and work them in good, stirring with a heavy wooden spoon, for a couple of minutes over a high heat. Add the cornmeal, ground ancho chilies, jalapenos, wine, coffee, soy sauce, fish sauce and tomatoes. Keep stirring as you bring it to a good boil, and then set aside until the beans are ready.

To finish cooking the beans, bring them back to a boil, then reduce the heat and let simmer for at least an hour.

When the beans are cooked to the point where their cooking liquid has thickened to gravy, pour it all into the big pot with the meat and everything else. Bring it gently to a boil, stirring the whole time with your wooden spoon to prevent scorching.

Let simmer 45 minutes, then open two bottles of beer, pour one into the chili and drink the other. Cover the pot, put it in the refrigerator and go to bed. Or, if you have a cookstove, transfer the chili to a bean pot (or Dutch oven), cover it with foil, put in your wood cookstove oven, and go to bed. One side effect of the second beer is that sooner or later during the night you'll have to get up. While you're up, throw enough wood on the cookstove fire so that the oven stays around 250°F.

Napkin art no. 810

If you've used a cookstove, come morning the chili will be ready. If you're using gas or electric, take the pot out of the refrigerator, and very gently, bring it to a boil, stirring almost constantly since at this point the chili can scorch easily.

Chili always tastes better the next day. For the most part Uncle Billy won't touch a bowl until it's been reheated two or three times, although if it's been in a woodstove overnight, he'll have a touch first thing in the morning, to benefit from what he, with a wink of his eye, refers to as the chili's "restorative" powers with the ladies. We don't know about that for sure, but will take his word on it.

Grandmother Alice's Red Flannel Hash

This recipe goes back to when Uncle Billy's mother would make hash for early morning hunter's breakfasts, or after all-night card games held around the dining room table when Jonny was just a little kid and Billy was still playing baseball.

She'd get up before light and using leftover meats, the remains of Thursday's New England boiled dinner, or Sunday's pork shoulder and baked potatoes, she'd make this hash. The beets were added because she considered them a tonic for the liver. To this day, Billy won't eat beets unless they're in his mother's Red Flannel Hash. Jonny's boys ask for it as often as his donuts; another legacy from his Grandmother Alice.

The only difference between Jonny's and his grandmother's recipe is that Jonny uses leftover barbeque meat instead of leftover Sunday supper roasts.

This recipe makes six whoppin' good portions.

- 1 pound leftover beef or pork
- 1 pound leftover baked potatoes, peeled
- 1/2 pound leftover cooked beets
- 1/2 stick margarine
- 1 pound Spanish onions, thinly sliced
- 1 heaping cup fresh parsley, finely chopped
- pinch nutmeg
- salt and white pepper to taste
- 6 eggs, poached
- barbeque sauce to taste

If you're using a food processor, pulse-chop the meat and put into a large mixing bowl. Then pulse chop the potatoes and then the beets, and combine with the chopped meat. Season with salt, pepper and nutmeg. If you don't have a food processor, as Alice certainly didn't, chop with a big knife on a cutting board. In either event, don't worry about trimming the meat too closely, as a bit of fat is needed to keep the hash moist.

Heat as large a cast iron skillet as you can find. The key word here is large: if your electric frying pan is bigger than your skillet, use that. While the pan or skillet is heating up chop the onions and the parsley by hand (the food processor will juice them too much) and set aside. When the skillet is hot, add the margarine and onions. Saute until the onions are translucent, and toss in everything else except the eggs and barbeque sauce.

Press down on the hash while it cooks with a large metal spatula. Lower the heat to medium and continue to cook 20-25 minutes on the stove, or 10 minutes on the stove then finish it off in a preheated 350°F oven, baking for 10-15 minutes. The oven method frees up the stovetop so you can begin poaching eggs. As the hash cooks, flip it three or four times, breaking it up with a spatula, into sections or pieces to keep it cooking evenly.

When the hash is done it will be browned, but not overly so. Portion onto plates, top with a poached egg, and keep the barbeque sauce handy. Blackburn's Maple Barbecue Sauce is good with this hash, even though he spells barbeque wrong.

Potlatch Gumbo

During his brief visit to Korea, Uncle Billy made the acquaintance of Trueman Stops, a Native American from Louisiana. Stops was only part of his real last name, the army couldn't fit his entire last name, Stops-At-Pretty-Places, on the breast pocket of his khakis.

Trueman and Billy, recognizing they had much in common (food among them) hit it off quick. On the day they met, Trueman was off to a potlatch. His instinct leading him by the nose, Billy followed his new friend to a party unlike any he had been to before. Close to 300 people were there, most of them U.S. servicemen, including a sizable contingent of Native Americans, as well as a handful of Koreans and a small busload of Greek nurses from a nearby Allied field hospital.

Two big pigs were turning on a spit, well attended by a fellow from Kansas. The pigs and the Kansan looked as if they'd been over the coals since late yesterday. Next to the pigs was one of those huge black witches' kettles. The coals under the kettle were hot and the full pot was simmering; its odor, Billy remembers, "A fragrance like none other," which is waxing poetic for him.

Trueman reached into his duffle bag and carefully removed a lump of seaweed, which he then unwrapped revealing two very large prawns. Trueman Stops-At-Pretty-Places dropped them into the black kettle. "Tonight," he said to Uncle Billy, "We eat the potlatch gumbo."

This recipe serves four easily, but it's so good you might want to triple it and invite over a bunch of friends to make a real potlatch.

- 2, 1-pound lobsters, boiled and picked clean, shells and meat set aside, or 50 crawfish tails, boiled and picked clean
- 1 pound hot link sausage, or Kielbasa, thick-sliced
- 1 large smoked ham hock
- 1 pound Spanish onions, thinly sliced
- 1 pound white Carolina rice, cooked
- 14-ounce can stewed tomatoes, in their juice
- 2 dozen oysters, shucked and with their liquor reserved
- 1 cup dark roux
- 1 cup dry white wine
- 4 green peppers, diced
- 4 stalks of celery, finely diced
- 6 ounces okra, fresh or frozen
- 1 carrot, rough-chopped
- 1/2 cup vegetable oil, or 1 stick margarine
- 1/4 cup fresh parsley, chopped, stalks saved
- 2 ounces cooking sherry or Port
- 1 ounce olive oil
- 2 heaping Tablespoons tomato paste
- 1 Tablespoon thyme leaves
- 1 Tablespoon hot Hungarian paprika
- 1 teaspoon black pepper
- 1 teaspoon white pepper
- 1/2 teaspoon file gumbo
- 1/2 teaspoon salt
- 1/2 teaspoon Cayenne pepper
- 4 bay leaves
- pinch ground cloves
- 1 leek, rinsed and cleaned, rough-chopped

☞ **Roux Ingredients**
- 2 cups all-purpose white flour
- 1 cup vegetable oil or 2 sticks margarine

About the roux: Roux is a thickening agent, used here to thicken a pork or shellfish stock. Okra and file gumbo are also thickeners, each contributing flavor as well as consistency. Uncle Billy doesn't like okra, so Jonny adds extra roux, keeping the okra in the vegetable bin.

Despite what you may have heard, a dark roux is not difficult to make. They can range in color from chestnut brown to almost black. The longer you cook the roux the darker it gets, and the greater the chance of it burning, so be careful. Jonny always makes a big batch and stores it, covered, in the refrigerator where it keeps for months.

Don't substitute butter for the vegetable oil or margarine, since it will burn. But if you can get some homemade lard, or bacon or goose fat, use that.

Heat up an iron skillet as hot as you can get it, put in the oil, margarine or whatever, when it's almost to the point of smoking up your house, whisk in half the flour, being careful to scrape the sides as well as you whisk. After two minutes whisk in the rest of the flour. Keep the heat high. After another two or three minutes it should be done. If dark flecks appear in your roux that means it is burning and you might have to start over again. Otherwise, set the roux aside to cool.

Split the lobster bodies in half lengthwise, using a cleaver. Remove and discard the stomach and other stuff that resides behind the eyes of the lobster. Heat two ounces of oil in a stainless steel or enamel stockpot over high heat. Saute the lobster parts for three minutes, then add the carrot, leek, half the paprika, one bay leaf, the ham hock, white wine, half the thyme, parsley stalks, tomatoes and their liquid, tomato paste and a quart of water. Bring to a boil, then reduce the heat and simmer for an hour, during which time you can prepare the other ingredients.

In another large pot saute the vegetables in the margarine for five minutes over high heat, stirring constantly. Add the remainder of the paprika as well as the remaining spices (except the file gumbo) while the vegetables cook. Whisk half the roux into this pot, then strain the lobster bouillon into this amalgam, using a heavy metal strainer or what restaurant people call a "China cap." When you're straining the bouillon and lobster parts, push down on them in the strainer with a potato masher or a heavy wooden spoon to extract all of their juice and flavor. Discard everything from the bouillon pot except for the ham hock, which goes into the gumbo pot.

Add what's left of the roux to the second pot and stir, so the resulting consistency is that of a thin gravy. Add the sausage and simmer another 15 minutes. Now cook the white rice.

Before you gather your guests around the table add to the pot the oysters with their liquor, sherry and lobster meat. Sprinkle the file gumbo and parsley on top, and bring the whole bowl to the table. Fluff up the rice in another bowl and spoon that wicked good gumbo over the top.

Red Beans and Rice

According to Uncle Billy, Jonny makes the best red beans and rice in the world. A mighty big claim; one that could precipitate a fatal accident in New Orleans, Jamaica or Little Havana be it made too loudly. It's all a matter of personal perspective, you understand. We suspect Billy's partiality to this red beans and rice has much to do with his fondness for sausage.

Billy always asks Jonny to cook up a batch of Red Beans and Rice come cold season, when he's feeling kind of mauger. Jonny's happy to oblige, especially since it's healthy fare for the kids as well.

- 12 ounces dry red kidney beans, or Japanese aduki beans*
- 2 ½ quarts water
- 2 ounces salt pork
- 2 cups white Carolina rice
- 2 Tablespoons corn oil
- 2 green bell peppers, coarsely chopped
- 1 large Spanish onion, coarsely chopped
- 1½ cup celery, finely chopped
- 1 supermarket bunch of mustard greens, coarsely chopped
- 1 4-ounce piece salt pork
- 1 pound hot link sausage or Cajun Andouille sausage, or Kielbasa (leftovers if you have them)
- 2 heaping Tablespoons fresh or dried parsley leaves, coarsely chopped
- 2 Tablespoons Hungarian paprika
- 2 Tablespoons dried thyme leaves
- 1 heaping Tablespoon dry, granulated garlic
- 4 dried bay leaves
- 1 heaping teaspoon black pepper
- 1 heaping teaspoon white pepper
- 1/8 teaspoon cayenne pepper
- 1 quart chicken or pork stock, or plain water
- 1 15-ounce can stewed tomatoes in their juice
- 1 12-ounce package frozen okra
- handful chives, freshly snipped
- Tabasco, or other hot sauce to taste

*Available in health food stores (Jonny says they're delicious, sweeter than kidney beans).

Bring the water, salt pork and beans to a strong boil in an uncovered pot. Then remove from the heat, cover and set aside for two hours. (If you have a wood cookstove and a sense of adventure, prepare the beans overnight in the cookstove.) Remember to hold onto the beans' cooking liquor.

Cook the rice according to the directions on the box and set aside.

In a heavy pot, saute the vegetables in corn oil over medium heat for five minutes, or until the vegetables are soft. Add the

Napkin art no. 74

salt pork and sausage, chopped or not, depending upon your preference. Stir in the spices and cook for two minutes, working it together with a large wooden spoon. Add the remaining ingredients, including the cooked beans and rice. Keep stirring it around with your spoon to prevent scorching. Turn the heat to low and simmer for 30 minutes. Add more liquid if necessary.

After half an hour, ladle portions into big bowls, making sure to include a good helping of meat. Now sprinkle chives on top, and keep that bottle of hot sauce close at hand. This dish is not guaranteed to cure colds, but it can make having one more tolerable.

Jonny's Downeast Fish Chowder

Livening up a favorite recipe is something Downeast barbeque is great for, and traditional recipes are no exception. In New England, people judge a chef by his chowder, and they've been known to judge a few quite harshly.

One story tells of a tar and feathering back in the late 1800s, in Kittery, Maine. Seems a chef there had garnished bowls of fish chowder with peanuts and okra. Had he served the soup to a genteel family with guests and chandeliers all about he probably would have been politely invited to leave. But he had the misfortune of serving the concoction to the annual gathering of Maine Civil War veterans who had served in Georgia — land of cotton and goober peas (peanuts).

Jonny learned to make a traditional chowder from his mother, who learned it from her mother, Alice. He's taken the family recipe and injected it with a little Downeast barbeque. The customers at Uncle Billy's love it. Still, Jonny gets nervous when he picks up the fragrance of hot tar on a summer's day.

This recipe will serve four hungry veterans of any war.

- 2 pounds finnan haddie, or any smoked fish or shellfish
- 1 pound Spanish onion, thinly sliced
- 1/2 gallon whole milk
- 2 pounds Maine russet potatoes, peeled and thickly sliced
- 2 whole stalks leeks, thoroughly cleaned and rough chopped
- 15-ounce can stewed tomatoes in their juice, chopped up
- 2 ounces dry Vermouth
- 2 teaspoons thyme leaves
- 1 teaspoon ground white pepper
- 1/2 teaspoon ground nutmeg
- 4 bay leaves
- 1/2 stick sweet butter
- 1 heaping Tablespoon dill leaves, freshly snipped
- 1/8 teaspoon salt

☞ For the Slurry
- 12-ounce can evaporated milk (or light cream)
- 3/4 cup white flour

Toss the onions, whole milk, potatoes, leeks, tomatoes and salt into a large, heavy pot. Do not cover. Bring it slowly to a boil, removing the top film as it forms, then turn down the heat to simmer. Leave off the cover and cook at this low heat until the potatoes are firm. Add the remaining ingredients except the butter, dill and slurry ingredients. Don't bother to cut the smoked fish, it will break up as the chowder simmers.

To make the slurry, whisk the evaporated milk and flour in a stainless steel bowl. As you whisk, add a small amount of the chowder liquid. This will prevent lumps, or what Uncle Billy unhappily calls "flavor buds." Pour the slurry into the chowder, stir well and continue simmering gently for another 15 minutes, stirring occasionally. If at any time the chowder appears to have curdled, which does happen from time to time, smooth it out by whisking in a little sour cream.

The chowder can be served now, but like Ranger Mel's chili, it's actually better the next day. Whenever you plan to serve it, first stir the half-stick of butter into the hot chowder and pour the whole concoction into a tureen, or directly into bowls, garnished with the dill and served with crusty rolls, homemade buttermilk biscuits, or better yet, fresh griddled ployes. After all, chowder (chaudiere) is a French original.

Sleepout Jonny's Barbeque Spaghetti

People always ask Jonny how he can barbeque spaghetti without it falling through the grill. Laughs aside, the real story behind barbeque spaghetti goes back to Uncle Billy's pool-shooting, baseball-playing days at Bates College.

Down in Lewiston on Lisbon Street, Uncle Billy came upon this spaghetti at an all-night, French-speaking B.Y.O.B. with plywood over the windows and a pool table downstairs, under the kitchen. The aroma of the spaghetti sauce that the proprietor, Sleepout Louie, was cooking, wafted downstairs. Right then Billy determined that he not only wanted a large bowl of the stuff, but the recipe as well.

"I'll bet you five bucks," he challenged Louie, "against you and your spaghetti sauce recipe." Then he racked up a game of eight-ball and invited the small French cook to break. Billy never got a shot in, Louie snookered him good. Although Billy lost the game, Louie gave him a consolation bowl of spaghetti — but no recipe.

Many years later, in Memphis, that same familiar smell grabbed Billy by his olfactory senses and just about dragged him into a nightclub called — you guessed it — Sleepout Louie's.

"Wanna rack 'em again?" Billy asked the short Frenchman behind the bar. This time Billy had the sharper eye.

This dish is quick and easy, so keep the ingredients around for when friends drop by. In this case, there's more than enough for six hungry people, with a little left over for breakfast the next morning.

- 2 pounds thin spaghetti
- 3 Tablespoons olive oil
- 1 pound Spanish onion, sliced
- 4 large red or green bell peppers, sliced
- 3 stalks of celery, diced
- 2 Tablespoons Hungarian paprika

- 1/4 cup fresh parsley, chopped
- 2 Tablespoons dried basil leaves
- 1 Tablespoon dried oregano
- 5 cloves garlic cloves, chopped up good
- 2 bay leaves
- pinch ground clove
- pinch cinnamon
- fresh ground black pepper to taste
- 1 cup dry white wine, cheap
- 1 pound leftover barbequed anything, chopped up
- 1 quart spaghetti sauce, store bought
- 3 anchovy fillets, mashed up
- 1/4 cup barbeque sauce
- 1/2 cup grated Romano or Parmesan cheese
- 8 ounces mushrooms sauteed in butter (optional)

Cook the spaghetti, real al dente, or follow the directions on the box. Drain, rinse and set aside in a colander. Heat the oil in a heavy saucepan or Dutch oven, and then throw in the chopped vegetables and the paprika. Saute until soft. Now add the parsley, dry spices, wine, the leftover barbeque and spaghetti sauce.

Cook this mixture for another 10-15 minutes — the longer the better — and if it gets too thick, add a little more white wine or water. Leave the spaghetti in the colander and set inside a large serving bowl and pour hot water over it. Then add the mashed anchovies, toss, drain, remove to a large serving bowl and pour on the sauce, adding the mushrooms if you decided to include them.

Pour the grated cheese into the pasta bowl, toss again, then serve it up with bottles of Chianti. Jonny likes to serve the barbeque sauce on the side, but some people pour it right into the bowl with the spaghetti sauce. A simple green salad with an oil and vinegar dressing and Jalapeno Cheesebread go well with this dish.

BREADS, SIDE DISHES & ACCOUTREMENTS

Catherine B. Hurley's Jalapeno Cheesebread
·
Damn Good Sweet Grilled Onions
·
Smoky Potatoes on the Grill
·
Joel's Back Bay Quick-Grilled Potatoes
·
Coal Roast Sweet Potatoes
·
Barbeque Billy Beans
·
Mother's Mountain Coleslaw
·
No Bean Shotgun Succotash
·
Corn on the Cob
·
Backwoods Green Tomato ChowChow

There's nothing better for soaking up barbeque sauce than a warm slice of jalapeno cheesebread. Few things go better with a rack of ribs than fresh corn on the cob and smoky potatoes; they're as natural together as roast turkey with cranberries and stuffing.

The recipes here will enhance your barbeque meal. They're easy to make, and a number of them use the coals you're already using.

If you, like many Mainers, go "up to camp" each summer (camp being a rented, owned or borrowed cabin up north, usually on a lake) many of these dishes, like the cheesebread, Backwoods Green Tomato ChowChow, Barbeque Billy Beans and a batch of Mother's Mountain Coleslaw can be made at home and taken to camp in a cooler. If Uncle Billy's traveling with you, though, better not seat him near the cooler.

Catherine B. Hurley

Catherine B. Hurley's Jalapeno Cheesebread

In the manner of barbeque joints the world over, fans of the grill are always wandering into the kitchen at Uncle Billy's Barbeque. There's no door to discourage them, and if there was a sign, which there isn't, they wouldn't read it so they just stroll on in with barbeque tales of their own to tell. They'd be sampling stuff from the chopping block, as well, if the cooks weren't so handy with cleavers. Most often the stories they spin are good ones, and sometimes they get woven into the lore that is as much a part of Uncle Billy's as the linoleum on the floor. Once in a while they even make it onto the menu, as is the case with this jalapeno cheesebread.

One day when Ms. Catherine was in command of the kitchen, a couple of South Texas Baptist bible salesmen strolled into her domain. They exchanged pleasantries and then the salesmen engaged Ms. Catherine in a discussion that became a debate on the state of the world. Just as abruptly as it began, the salesmen turned from the kitchen and sat down at the nearest booth where they ordered double orders of ribs, brisket, chicken and sausage. They spoke not another word, not to Ms. Catherine, not to Jonny who wandered in and wandered out, not even to each other. They ate it all, cleaned off every rib, every Billy Bean, chicken bone, sausage and cornbread. Then one of them wrote on a napkin and showed it to the other, who nodded his head yes. While one paid the tab, the other got up and tacked the napkin to the wall near the phone.

Things got busy and soon everyone forgot about the napkin. It stayed tacked to the wall for about a month until one day when

Jonny, who wasn't paying attention to something someone was telling him on the phone, noticed the napkin with its drawings and vague instructions.

It took a few days of tinkering, but this is what Jonny and the lovely Ms. Catherine came up with. It goes especially well with an order or two of barbequed brisket, and does an admirable job soaking up the drippings from just about any meal.

This recipe makes 2, 6 x 9-inch loaves.

- 3/4 pound sharp cheddar cheese, grated
- 1½ ounces jalapeno peppers, finely minced
- 3/4 ounce dry baker's yeast
- 1 ounce sugar
- 3 cups water (plus 1/2 cup warm water)
- 3 Tablespoons melted margarine
- 1/2 cup minced onions
- 1 teaspoon salt
- 1 teaspoon cumin
- 1 egg
- 1/2 cup dried milk
- 5½ cups flour

Mix together the cheese and peppers in a bowl and set aside. In another bowl dissolve the yeast and sugar in 1/2 cup of warm water (about 120°F) and set aside.

In a very large bowl combine the yeast-sugar-water mixture with the three cups of water and melted margarine, and then add the onions. Let it sit for five minutes before adding the salt, cumin, egg and dried milk. Mix it well with a large spoon. Now stir in the peppers and cheese.

Gradually pour 3½ cups of the flour into the bowl, stirring until it becomes difficult, then put the dough on a dry, well-floured surface and knead for about 10 minutes, adding the rest of the flour as you work the dough. Knead until you can stick your finger into the dough, and it pulls out clean, not sticky. Put the dough back in the bowl and cover; set it in a warm place for approximately one hour, at which point the dough should have doubled in volume.

Dump the dough onto a floured surface, punch it down and let it rest for 10 minutes. Cut it into two equal pieces and shape into loaves. Place the dough into two greased loaf pans. Make a light cut lengthwise along the top of each loaf. Set the loaf pans in a warm place for 30-45 minutes, and let the dough rise a second time.

The dough will almost double in volume, rising an inch or two above the loaf pan. Bake in a pre-heated 325°F oven 45 minutes to an hour. This bread browns easily, so don't be fooled into thinking it's done just because the top is brown. It's ready when you can stick a toothpick in and remove it clean.

Remove the bread from the pans, slather with margarine and cool on racks before you slice it. The loaves can be frozen after baking, as long as they're well-wrapped.

Damn Good Sweet Grilled Onions

Uncle Billy divides food into two categories: food he makes and loves to eat, and food someone else (most notably Nephew Jonny) makes that he loves to eat. Most fall into the second category, but here's one Uncle Billy likes best when he cooks it himself.

The recipe for this particular accoutrement came about simply enough. Billy was visiting an old card-playing crony at another buddy's camp up towards Rangeley Lake. There was a gang of people there; Billy only knew two of them when he arrived, but a common love of food, beverage and cards brought him five more friends — and a pocketful of money by the end of the week.

One of the new guys, Jim Sweet, drew himself out of the game for a while. Just as Billy began to wonder what had happened to him, agreeable aromas began making their way from the brick barbeque rig around back. Minutes later, out came a platter of huge venison steaks and a plate of onions that had been cooked over the fire with the venison. Somewhere about halfway into his second or third helping of onions (and towards the end of his second steak) Billy was asked what he thought of the onions.

"Damn good," Billy said, then commenced to cleaning his plate.

The name stuck. Billy still heads north to the camp once or twice a year for refills of venison and a jug or two of homemade. Jim was just passing through that first time and hasn't been by since, so now Billy makes the onions himself, and he makes a lot of them.

- 1 medium Spanish onion per person, peeled
- 2 teaspoons butter per onion
- 1/4 teaspoon Voodoo Jerk Slather Sauce

Butter the center of a piece of aluminum foil large enough to wrap around the onion (about 12 x 8 inches). Cut off the ends of the onion and make a third cut around the middle, as if you were cutting big onion rings. Place the remainder of the butter between the two halves of the onion. Here, if you feel the urge, is where you can add the Voodoo Jerk Slather Sauce. It's up to you, just remember to do something Uncle Billy would find blasphemous: be temperate with the stuff. Tasty as it is, it can generate heat while sitting on a shelf in a deep freeze.

Join together the two halves of buttered (and slathered) onion, wrap tightly in the foil, and put it on a medium-hot grill for 45 minutes, turning once or twice. When they're done, the onions should be soft and lightly browned, but not charred. If they're still crunchy in the middle, remember to cook them a little longer next time. Should they flare up while cooking, move them to a cooler part of the grill.

Cooking the onions this way makes them sweet and mild in taste, so they can go with almost any meat dish, particularly beef and pork ribs. Some people like them on barbeque pork sand-wiches, too, which isn't the worst idea we've ever heard. They're addictive, though, so don't worry about making too many. Besides, if a small herd of vegetarians should sneak into your party, they'll go after a plate of these onions faster than you can say tofu. Then you can get back to the serious business of eating ribs, forking up onions and dealing the next hand.

Smoky Potatoes on the Grill

This is as easy a recipe as you'll ever find. If you can identify a potato and light a barbeque fire, you can make these potatoes. They're good with just about everything.

It doesn't matter what wood or chips you use. Whether it's whisky- or water-soaked corn cob, alder, or fruitwood chips, the potatoes will soak up that good smoky flavor like a sponge.

One note about the sea salt listed with the ingredients: Despite the fact that Maine has some 3,000 miles of seacoast, it's not like you can wander down to the rocks and scoop up a handful. In fact, most packaged sea salt comes from the Persian Gulf and Caribbean Islands, making it pretty expensive. We usually pick up a box of kosher salt at the supermarket for a fraction of the price.

- 2 medium Red Bliss potatoes per person (better yet, use new Maine potatoes)
- 1 plus teaspoon olive oil
- sea (or kosher) salt
- fresh black pepper, to taste

Pour a teaspoon and a bit more of olive oil onto a piece of aluminum foil large enough to wrap around two potatoes (about 12 x 8-inches). Pour a few tablespoons of salt into a small dish, then grind on a little fresh pepper. Roll the potatoes in the olive oil on the foil until coated, then lightly roll them in the salt and pepper. Shake off any excess salt and pepper and place the potatoes next to each other on the foil. Wrap the foil tightly around the potatoes and place them on a fairly hot part of a medium-hot grill for 45 minutes to an hour, turning them once or twice. You can substitute Maine Russets or Idaho bakers, but figure only one per person and wrap them one to a piece of foil.

The skin of the potato will be blackened but not blistered, and will taste delicious with anything from barbeque sauce to sour cream and chives.

While you have the fire smoking, and if you happen to have a big bag of potatoes sitting in the root cellar, cook up a whole mess of potatoes to use in your favorite potato salad recipe for some great, smoky-tasting potato salad. Or, cut them while hot, sprinkle with vodka and serve with creme fraiche and Ossetra caviar.

*Saturday night at Uncle Billy's: napkin art,
Chris the dashing waiter, plates of ribs
and pitchers of beer.*

Joel's Back Bay Quick-Grilled Potatoes

Jonny's old friend and fellow restaurateur, Joel, makes these potatoes over at his restaurant, the Back Bay Grill, northside across the bridge in Portland proper. These are the only potatoes served in Joel's grill room. Jonny and Joel will sit in the kitchen and talk for hours with nothing but a plate of these potatoes and a pitcher of martinis, that's how good they are.

- 1 dozen medium-size Maine Russet potatoes, scrubbed
- olive oil
- kosher salt
- fresh black pepper

Boil the potatoes with their jackets on in salted water until just barely cooked, about 10 minutes, then drain and set aside to cool. When they're cool enough to handle, peel with a paring knife and slice lengthwise into pieces 1-inch thick. Sprinkle with salt and pepper, brush with olive oil and place on a hot grill. After two minutes flip them, cook for another couple of minutes and serve.

Napkin art no. 911

Coal Roast Sweet Potatoes

If you thought Smoky Potatoes on the Grill was easy to prepare, you'll love this one.

- sweet potatoes
- butter
- kosher salt
- pepper
- nutmeg, freshly ground

Wash as many sweet potatoes as you plan to use, then dry them and wrap in aluminum foil. Bury them in a bed of hot coals and cook for an hour.

Using long-handled tongs, remove the potatoes from the coals and cool for a few minutes; remove the foil, slice the potatoes lengthwise, slather with melted butter, sprinkle with salt, pepper and the nutmeg, and serve.

Napkin art no. 119

Barbeque Billy Beans

Believe it or not, Uncle Billy's SouthSide Barbeque enjoys the devoted patronage of a sizeable contingent of vegetarians. They sit at the counter and order big plates of Barbeque Billy Beans, coleslaw and cornbread, much to the amusement of Billy, who likes to sit down next to them with a big plate of ribs. Billy considers vegetarian-conversions his missionary duty.

As good as they are, these beans aren't difficult to make, they just take time, so you might as well make up a big batch. This recipe yields more than a gallon.

- 2 pounds navy or pea beans
- 1 gallon water
- 1 pound Spanish onions, thinly sliced
- 3 Tablespoons vegetable oil, or bacon fat
- 3 Tablespoons dry mustard, mixed with 1 cup of water
- 1/2 cup Barbados molasses
- 1/2 cup brown sugar
- 1/2 cup barbeque sauce
- 3 Tablespoons marjoram leaves
- 2 Tablespoons granulated garlic
- 1 Tablespoon ground cumin
- 1 Tablespoon back pepper
- 1 Tablespoon ground coriander
- 1 Tablespoon soy sauce
- 1/2 teaspoon ground nutmeg
- 1/2 teaspoon Worcestershire Sauce
- 6 bay leaves
- pinch ground cloves
- 1 smoked ham hock (optional)

Soak the beans overnight in a large metal (but not stainless steel) kettle. The next day bring the beans to a rip-roaring boil in the uncovered kettle (or better yet, in a pressure cooker), and boil for five minutes. Remove from the heat, cover, and leave them to swell, which will take at least an hour, although two hours is better.

While the beans sit, chop the onions and saute in the oil, in a hot skillet, until they start to brown. Remove from the heat and set aside.

After the beans have swelled, mix in the sauteed onions. Stir in the dry mustard and water slurry, then add everything else, stirring again. If you're using a pressure cooker, cover and bring to a boil, then cook for an hour. In a kettle, bring the mixture to a boil, uncovered, then reduce the heat and simmer for two hours, stirring occasionally to prevent scorching.

If you have a wood cookstove, you might consider baking the beans overnight.

No matter how you cook Barbeque Billy Beans, they're always best when reheated. In the restaurant, people season them further with everything from mustard to Louisiana hot sauce. There's no reason not to, particularly if there is some fresh-baked bread around to soak up the gravy.

Mother's Mountain Coleslaw

For Uncle Billy's favorite coleslaw, Jonny uses the best cabbage he can find, which in his opinion comes from Alewife's Farm in his hometown of Cape Elizabeth. The Jordans, who own the farm, know everything there is to know about cabbage. They ought to, their family has been growing cabbage out on the Cape since back when the Massoit Indians were waiting for the Pilgrims to crash into the Massachusetts shoreline.

Not everyone is fortunate enough to live near Alewife's Farm. That being the case, just make sure you get the best cabbage you can find. Get a big one.

This concoction owes its name to one of the ingredients, Mother's Mountain Mustard, which comes from nearby Falmouth, where, by the way, there's not a mountain to be seen.

- 1, 2-pound cabbage
- 1 pound Spanish onions, peeled, rough chopped and pureed
- 1/2 cup cider vinegar
- 1/4 cup granulated sugar
- 3 cloves garlic, chopped and mashed
- 1½ teaspoons ground celery seed
- 1 Tablespoon kosher salt
- 1 teaspoon ground black pepper
- 1 cup vegetable oil
- 2 ounces whole caraway seeds
- 1½ cups mayonnaise
- 1/2 jar (3 ounces) Mother's Mountain Mustard

Core and quarter the cabbage, then slice as thinly as possible using a sharp chef's knife or the slicer-blade attachment of your food processor. Mix together the cabbage and onions in a large bowl, toss with the cider vinegar, sugar, garlic, celery seed, salt and pepper. In a heavy saucepan bring the oil and caraway seeds to a good boil. Pour it over the contents of the bowl, being careful not to splash yourself — we're talking boiling oil here. Add the mayonnaise and mustard, and toss well. Serve hot or cold.

No Bean Shotgun Succotash

If you were a teenager in a rural town, or for that matter, if you've ever been a farmer, you already know all about what we in Maine refer to as pinchin'. There is something of an understanding between the parties involved: as long as you don't take too much, don't make a ruckus, wake the dog or trample the vegetation, and, most importantly, as long as you aren't stupid enough to get caught, the farmer exercises some tolerance. This, of course, varies from farmer to farmer.

Nephew Jonny, as a young teenager, got a bit carried away anticipating a big feed at Grandmother Alice's, and went about his freelance harvesting with more exuberance than sense. Along about his third trip to the same farmer's garden, having gathered corn, tomatoes and green peppers on the first two trips, the farmer's old breechlock side-by-side brought Jonny's gathering expedition to a halt by way of two 12-gauge rounds of rock salt. Jonny returned home with a sore backside and an empty bushel basket, which is why there are no lima beans in the succotash. Billy's just as happy, since he doesn't much care for lima beans.

This will make a gallon or so of succotash.

- 2 dozen ears fresh corn on the cob, or frozen kernels
- 2 quarts water, lightly salted
- 2 ounces salt pork, cubed
- 2 cups Spanish onion, peeled and diced
- 1 cup flour
- 2 cups cabbage, thinly sliced and diced
- 1/4 cup fresh basil leaves, chopped
- 2 teaspoons thyme leaves
- 2, 14-ounce cans peeled tomatoes in their liquid, diced

- 1 cup flour
- 1 cup green bell peppers, diced
- 1 cup celery, diced
- 8 ounces leftover barbequed pork shoulder (or 1 large ham hock)
- 2 teaspoons salt
- 1/2 teaspoon Worcestershire Sauce
- 1/2 teaspoon black pepper
- 1/8 teaspoon mace
- 2 whole cloves
- 2 dashes Tabasco sauce
- 1 bay leaf
- 1/2 cup parsley, chopped

Cut the corn from the ears, put in a bowl and set aside. Bring the water and salt pork to a boil, add the corn and blanch for five minutes, then drain the water and remove the salt pork. In a large heavy pot, gently saute the salt pork in the oil for 8-10 minutes over low heat. To this pot, add the onions and cook five minutes, or until transparent. Stir in the flour and cook gently for a minute. Add the rest of the ingredients and bring to a light boil, then reduce the heat and simmer 45 minutes, adding water as necessary.

Pour the succotash into a serving bowl, garnish with the chopped parsley, place on the table next to Flank Steak Weekend, and see if anyone even notices the lima beans are missing.

FREEZING SUMMER CORN

Have the kids shuck the corn as soon as possible after picking (or pinchin'). Blanch for five minutes in boiling water to which a couple tablespoons of sugar have been added. Then drain, cut off the kernels and store the corn in the freezer in zip-top plastic bags. Be sure to squeeze the air out of the bags before sealing. Come February, you'll be glad you did. It might not bring back summer, but close your eyes and you can pretend.

Corn on the Cob

In the succotash recipe we mentioned pinchin' as a teenage harvesting method that gives both parties, the pincher and the pinched, a bit of pleasure when the moon is dark and nothing good is playing at the movie theater. It's one of those simple pleasures of living in the country. Pinchin' corn, however, can be a one-sided good time had by the farmer alone.

One of the more beautiful sights in rural America, whether you're driving through or flying above, are the farms with hundreds of acres of planted crops — corn, wheat, cabbage, whatever — growing in long furrowed rows. As the summer winds down, the corn reaches heights tall enough to conceal even a pinchin' party from the Boston Celtics (though they ought to be ashamed of themselves for doing it). Thing is, more often than not those mile-long, eight-foot rows of corn are meant to feed cows come winter, not people.

Go to a grange hall supper and the loudest laughter often comes from the corner where the farmers are telling of the college boys from the city, or the counselors from the nearby summer camp, nursing rock salt burns and breaking their teeth on the cow corn they stole but won't be able to eat. This recipe calls for people corn.

- fresh ears of sweet corn
- salt
- sugar
- butter

If the corn has been sitting at the market for a couple days rather than coming straight from the garden or farm stand, blanch for 30 seconds, husks and all, in a large kettle of boiling water to which a little salt and sugar has been added. Then remove from the water.

If your corn is fresh from the garden, start here. Pull back the husk, and with a nylon bristle brush slather on melted butter. Pull the husk back up and toss the corn on a medium-hot grill over an indirect heat, cover and cook for 45 minutes.

If you prefer, don't pull the husk back before you place the corn on the grill. Rather, remove it entirely, don't add any butter, wrap in foil, put the corn right in the coals and cook for 15 minutes. Watch it carefully with this method, as cooking times will vary with hotter or cooler fires and corn size.

Either way, flip the corn two or three times while it cooks. The corn may be slightly charred in places, but that's fine as long as it isn't burnt.

Backwoods Green Tomato ChowChow

ChowChow is a great way to clean out your garden at the end of the growing season, which in Maine comes a damn sight too soon for most folks. When Nephew Jonny is feeling Francophilic, he calls the dish *Fin de la Jardin ChowChow*. The first time he heard this, Uncle Billy, who, when his gout is acting up, calls his nephew, "That little French bastid," always calls it by its real name, though for the last five or six years he's been trying to find a Celtic equivalent.

This recipe makes one gallon of ChowChow, and we recommend that you don't cut it one bit, even if you're just having a few friends over to dinner that night. It keeps well in the root cellar, and when there's snow on the ground as there is most times in northern Maine, it makes for a pleasant reminder of the brief summer months.

- 3 pounds green tomatoes, cut into 1/8-inch slices
- 6 red bell peppers, seeded and finely diced
- 1 small head of cabbage, finely grated
- 1 small head of celery, finely diced
- 2 pounds whole garden onion, stalks and bulbs, finely chopped
- 1/2 pound any kind of green beans, chopped
- 5 Tablespoons kosher salt
- 3 cups cider vinegar
- 2 cups white granulated sugar
- 1/2 cup molasses
- 1/4 cup hot chiles, rough chopped
- 3 Tablespoons turmeric
- 2 teaspoons ground celery seed
- 2 teaspoons white pepper
- 1 Tablespoon granulated garlic
- 1 teaspoon cumin seed
- 1 teaspoon ground allspice
- 6 whole cloves
- 2 Tablespoons dry mustard
- 1½ cups white flour

Put all the vegetables in a large crock or in a stainless steel pot with three tablespoons of the salt and four cups of cold water. Cover and let stand overnight.

The next morning drain off the water, add the remaining ingredients (except the mustard and flour), plus three cups of cold water and bring to a boil, uncovered. Reduce heat and simmer for 15 minutes.

In a small bowl make a slurry of the flour, dry mustard and a cup of cold water, whisking until smooth. When the slurry is ready, mix it into the ChowChow, stirring all the while. Bring the ChowChow back to a boil, then remove from the heat and pour into warm, sterilized canning jars and put it down cellar, or in the refrigerator where it will keep for up to three months. The best thing about Jonny's ChowChow is that it's good with barbequed anything.

Rubs, Bastes, Slathers & Sauces

Uncle Billy's Own Barbeque Sauce
•
A Quart of Jonny's Improvisational Eating Sauce
•
Killer Gene's Tar Heel Vinegar Sauce
•
Georges Henri's Homebrew Barbeque Baste
•
Sebago Pig & Poultry Rub
•
Black Pan Fish Mix
•
Heifer Pat Down
•
Ram Island Lamb Rub

More arguments start over barbeque sauce than anything else having to do with this cuisine. It's regional; it's personal; for all we know it may have religious significance. We suggest you experiment a bit, and when you find a sauce recipe that works for your taste buds, don't tinker with it too much, you'll just be messing up a good thing. Trust us.

Barbeque sauce recipes usually come with ingredient lists longer than most kids' Christmas list. Making a sauce can be intimidating, even if the cooking instructions are simple. Fortunately, there are some good sauces on the supermarket shelves, and others can be bought by mail. We've provided you with all three options — you can make Uncle Billy's Own Barbeque Sauce from scratch, doctor up store-bought varieties using Jonny's Improvisational Sauce recipe, or you can pick up the phone or drop a line, to some of the folks listed in the resource chapter at the end of the book.

You need to be aware of some distinctions, though. The sauce mixture you apply at the table to already-cooked foods is called an *eating sauce* or, to confuse matters, just *sauce*. What's applied to the barbeque as it cooks is a *baste*, and the spice mix massaged in before cooking is called a *rub*. They can all be made up ahead of time and kept either in the refrigerator (the sauces and bastes) or in jars on the pantry shelf (the rubs). That way they're always handy for impromptu barbeques, which often turn out to be the best kind. Uncle Billy even takes a little jar of the Black Pan Fish Mix with him when he goes fishing in case he's lucky enough to meet someone with a skillet and a couple of fish to fry.

Uncle Billy's Own Barbeque Sauce

Folks who make barbeque sauce are as secretive about their recipes as moonshiners are about the locations of their stills. Many a cook will ask his closest friend to leave the kitchen when it comes time to cook up a fresh batch of sauce.

In fact, when Stewart Blackburn of Stache Foods, the maker of the Blackburn's Maple Barbeque Sauce that Jonny enjoys so much, starts to work on a fresh batch, Jonny is always invited to stay and taste.

However, when the mixing of this and that is underway, it is quietly suggested that he retire to another room. That's how proprietary this sort of thing is. Friendship's friendship, all right, but sauce, now that's really special.

Jonny takes no offense, just as Stewart takes none when Jonny has him leave the room while mixing a batch of Death By Chocolate Dessert Sauce, even though they make it in Stewart's commerical kitchen at Stache Foods.

Jonny serves Uncle Billy's Own (hot) and Blackburn's (mild) eating sauces at Uncle Billy's Barbeque. Some customers, getting right into the spirit of things, slather a little of Blackburn's with a little Uncle Billy's atop their brisket, ribs, shoulders, chicken, brisket, fish, chili, cheesebread — everything.

This recipe makes a gallon and a half of sauce, with enough left over for a batch of Barbeque Billy Beans. You can store covered jars of the sauce in the refrigerator where it will keep for months, or on the pantry in canning jars.

This potent concoction is an eating sauce, *not* a cooking sauce (or baste). Set it on the table and let your guests doctor their meals any way they please.

- 2½ quarts water
- 12-ounce can Moxie soda
- 1/4 cup Hungarian hot paprika
- 1/4 cup granulated onion powder
- 1/8 cup ground oregano leaf
- 2 Tablespoons ground cumin
- 1 ounce bittersweet chocolate bits
- 3 teaspoons black pepper
- 3 teaspoons granulated garlic
- 1 Tablespoon crushed red pepper flakes
- 2 Tablespoons salt
- 2 teaspoons ground anise
- 2 Tablespoons cayenne pepper
- 1 Tablespoon ground coriander
- 1/2 teaspoon ground celery seed
- 1/2 teaspoon ground nutmeg
- 2 dashes allspice
- dash dry ginger
- small can frozen orange juice concentrate
- 2, 6-ounce cans tomato paste
- 5 cups cider vinegar
- 1/2 cup Barbados molasses
- 2 Tablespoons soy sauce
- 1 Tablespoon Worcestershire sauce
- 1/4 cup vegetable oil
- 1/4 cup red wine, cheap
- 1/4 cup black coffee, old
- 2 Tablespoons prepared horseradish

In a small bowl, combine all the dry spices with one pint of the water and the Moxie to make a paste. The best tool to use is a whisk. In a large, heavy enamel or stainless steel pot bring two quarts of water to a boil then whisk in the paste. Add the rest of the ingredients to the pot, stirring continuously until it boils again. Reduce heat immediately and let simmer for 15 minutes; remove from the burner and let cool. Pour the sauce into plastic jugs, cover and store in a cool place.

A Quart of Jonny's Improvisational Eating Sauce

We don't blame you one bit if you don't feel like making a huge pot of from-scratch barbeque sauce, especially when you're hungry for barbeque and the last canning jar of sauce became an almost-forgotten birthday present for the neighbor down the street who always remembers yours.

No problem, just run to the store and pick up a jar of K.C.'s Masterpiece barbecue sauce, which is what Uncle Billy does when his nephew is out of town, and spruce it up a bit with the list below. If your market doesn't carry K.C.'s, pick another, this is, after all, an improvisational adventure.

- 2 Tablespoons dry granulated onions
- 16 ounces K.C.'s Masterpiece (or other store-bought sauce)
- 1 cup water
- 1/2 cup cider vinegar
- 1/8 cup red wine, cheap
- 1/8 cup reconstituted lemon juice
- 1/2 cup brown sugar, or honey
- 1 Tablespoon salt
- 2 teaspoons Tabasco
- 1 teaspoon black pepper
- 3 shakes Worcestershire sauce

Combine the ingredients in a large pot and bring to a boil, stirring regularly. After 15 minutes, remove from the stove and pour into a jar or other container. Use right away or store in the refrigerator.

Killer Gene's Tar Heel Vinegar Sauce

If this sauce takes you more than five minutes to make, from start to finish, you're either doing something wrong or you're spending entirely too much time taking an inventory of your liquor cabinet.

At the restaurant, Killer Gene's sauce goes on pulled and chopped pork shoulder sandwiches. This recipe makes a pint, which is enough for an entire Tar Heel pig roast. It will keep for months refrigerated.

Jonny also mixes this sauce with equal parts of tomato juice to wash his dog after one of her semi-annual skunk meetings. Hopefully, your dog has more sense than his and you can save the sauce for eating.

- 2½ cups cider vinegar
- 1 cup sugar
- 1/4 cup Tabasco sauce
- 1/4 cup pickle brine
- 1 Tablespoon granulated garlic
- 2 teaspoon salt
- 2 teaspoons ground black pepper

Combine the ingredients in a clean jar with a tight-fitting lid and shake well before each use.

A word about Killer Gene. Hailing from the Tar Heel state of North Carolina, Gene boxed in the basement ring under Jonny's kitchen when the restaurant first opened. The ceiling was a little low and the ring wasn't regulation, but Gene had a jab and hook combo that cracked ribs and loosened teeth with frightening regularity. He liked to come upstairs, chat with Jonny, eat pork shoulder sandwiches and mix up batches of this sauce to put on them. To those who knew him outside the ring, a sweeter kinder man never lived.

Georges Henri's Homebrew Barbeque Baste

Back in the days when Prohibition made certain beverages difficult to find, Jonny's grandfather, Georges Henri, newly-arrived from Quebec, found that the wording of the 18th Amendment had little effect on his thirst for such things. Luckily, he had a homebrew beer recipe that not only kept his whistle well whetted, but also earned him a certain profitable notoriety his among neighbors and the patrons of his barber shop/pool hall.

Jonny still uses the homebrew recipe, but for expediency's sake, he substitutes a bottle of Guinness Stout for the original barber shop concoction.

- 1 cup water boiled with 1 packet of spruce gum, or 1/4 cup white Retsina wine, plus 1/4 cup water
- 12-ounce bottle Guiness Stout, or homebrew
- 2 cups cider vinegar
- 3/4 cup Barbados molasses
- 1/4 cup melted margarine
- 1/4 cup any eating barbeque sauce
- 1 Tablespoon granulated garlic
- good shake Tabasco sauce
- 1 Tablespoon salt
- 1 teaspoon ground black pepper
- 3 shakes Worcestershire sauce

Spruce gum is fairly easy to find in New England, but if you're not in New England or don't care to look, it can be ordered from L.L. Bean from anywhere. White Retsina wine has the same sort of pine flavor and is a more than adequate substitute.

Boil the water and spruce gum in a small saucepan until the water is reduced almost by half. Remove from the stove. After it has cooled some, pour the liquid into a larger pot and add the other ingredients. (Give the gum to the kids, who will think it a treat.)

Simmer five minutes and it's ready to slather on the meat.

This baste will keep indefinitely, as long as it's covered and refrigerated. The molasses gives it a good Downeast flavor, one that for comparison's sake, contrasts with the traditional Southern bastes, which are not quite as sweet.

A paintbrush with nylon bristles and a long wooden handle makes a great barbeque basting tool. Restaurant supply and paint stores stock them. Feel free to improvise, just make sure the handle of whatever you use keeps your hands from spending time over the coals.

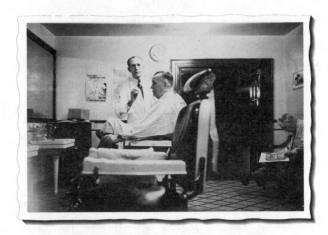

Georges Henri at his barber shop
— homebrew in the back room
and pool tables downstairs.

Sebago Pig & Poultry Rub

Nephew Jonny, Uncle Billy and some of their friends were up to camp on Sebago Lake visiting relatives when, as usually happens, Jonny was designated that evening's cook. He was in the kitchen, pondering possible dinner entrees, when a bunch of chickens burst through the screen door, chased by an assortment of children, angry adults and one wet dog. The chickens headed for the pantry and ran straight into the spice shelf. An open jar of Oriental Five Spice Powder fell down, covering the chickens, pantry, dog and one of the kids with a pretty liberal dose of the spice powder.

A good-sized mess was the result. Jonny lost his characteristic laissez-fare attitude, and since the kid belonged to a relative and everyone was partial to the dog, dinner that night was arrived at by deductive reasoning — it would be chicken.

To this day Jonny swears the story is true, and what's more, he said those chickens, all tossed with Oriental Five Spice Powder, were the best he'd ever eaten. Which is exactly why he puts it in his Sebago Pig & Poultry Rub. There's enough here for a pound of rub. Store it on a shelf (minding the kids and dogs); it'll come in handy time and time again.

- 3½ ounces granulated garlic
- 3 ounces Hungarian paprika
- 2½ ounces granulated sugar
- 2½ ounces Oriental Five Spice Powder
- 1½ ounces salt
- 1½ ounces black pepper
- 1/2 ounce ground marjoram
- 1/2 ounce ground anise
- 1/4 ounce ground sage
- 1/8 ounce ground allspice
- 1/8 ounce ground ginger

Black Pan Fish Mix

This mix works on most fish and shellfish, and is essential for Schyla Jean's Jewel Island Shrimp Feast, which not only uses shrimp from the Gulf of Maine, but a real black pan (cast iron skillet) as well. You can't get much more Downeast.

The essential things to remember when using this mix, no matter what fish you're fixing, is that the pan must be very large and very hot, the fish or shellfish should be coated first in the mix, then in melted margarine, and then put into the very hot pan, which will sear in the natural juices.

This yields a half-pound of mix.

- 2½ ounces hot Hungarian paprika
- 2 ounces granulated garlic
- 1½ ounces salt
- 1 ounce black pepper
- 1/2 ounce white pepper
- 1/2 ounce ground thyme
- 1/4 ounce ground nutmeg
- 1/4 ounce ground bay leaf
- 1/8 ounce cayenne pepper
- 1/4 ounce ground ginger
- 1/8 ounce ground cumin

Heifer Pat Down

There was a fellow down around Sanford, Maine who claimed to get veal-tender beef from his 18-month old steers. Many tried to learn his secret, but few, maybe only one, ever got it out of him — that one being Uncle Billy, of course.

They met at Maine's annual fall party, the Common Ground Fair, near a booth where a local smokehouse was exhibiting and giving away samples. "Damn chewy," the farmer overheard Billy say between his slipping uppers and lowers. Next thing Uncle Billy knows, someone's got him gently by the elbow and is leading him a few paces south of the exhibit. The farmer pulled a stick of jerky from his inside coat pocket and handed it to Billy, who without considering his mamma Alice's lessons about taking food from strangers, popped it into his mouth. Despite it being smoked and jerked dry, the meat was tender through and through.

The farmer, having been stationed south during his stint in the Navy, was a man who appreciated good barbeque. Uncle Billy took him down to Jonny's place the next day. His eyes watered he was so happy. He ate a couple pork shoulder sandwiches, a rack and a half of bastid ribs and half a barbequed chicken, slathering Uncle Billy's Own Barbeque Sauce on everything, even the Mother's Mountain Coleslaw. Knowing his uncle's guest was a beef farmer, Jonny kept offering him brisket, which he kept refusing, ever so politely. "No slight to your cooking," he said meaning to be complimentary, "But unless it was grown by me, beef is too tough to chew."

Billy used that as an opening to ask him how he got such tender meat from full-grown beef cattle. His new friend didn't answer the question but asked Jonny to pass him some more barbeque sauce, which he then slathered on his corn bread. "What do you put in that sauce to flavor it so?" he asked Jonny. As his nephew was beginning to open his mouth, Uncle Billy kicked his shin hard but quiet. "Old, old family recipe," he said, "Jonny loses his inheritance should either of us give it out." The farmer was disappointed, but he shouldn't have been, Billy was just getting started. They talked about rib joints and chilies they had eaten. Turned out the farmer knew Ranger Mel. Billy was truly happy to have found a new friend so close to home.

The farmer must have known Billy's joy was genuine and his friendship worth having because he huddled the three of them around the countertop and told them the secret. "I rub those Heifers but good." When Jonny asked what he rubbed them with, meaning with what spices, the farmer said, "My hands son, I massage them every day of their lives."

Few beef farmers have the time or the inclination to lay their cattle on the table and therapeutically work the tensions out of their critters' untanned hides. That being the case, buying from quality meat counters, blending the natural flavors with good rubs, bastes, slathers and sauces, and cooking it low and slow is still the best way to go.

Among the many things Jonny learned about rubs from his old chef-mentor, Marcel, was how well lavender complements beef. When Jonny formulated the spices for a beef rub, lavender was the first ingredient he included.

This recipe will make about a pound of Heifer Pat Down. Just mix the ingredients together and store on your pantry shelf.

- 3½ ounces cumin
- 3½ ounces granulated garlic
- 2½ ounces salt
- 2 ounces black pepper
- 1½ ounces coriander
- 1 ounce dry mustard
- 1/2 ounce ground anise
- 1/2 ounce ground marjoram
- 1/2 ounce ground lavender leaves*
- 1/8 ounce ground cloves
- 1/4 ounce allspice
- 1/4 ounce ground thyme

*Four possible sources of lavender leaves: Your garden, a well-stocked health-food store, Pendery's catalog, or pick through a basket of potpourri.

Ram Island Lamb Rub

Ram Island Farm was once an estate too large to be called a gentleman's farm — country-squire estate might do it better justice. As well as flocks of sheep and many, many gardens of herbs and flowers, Ram Island Farm was home to Guido DeSantos. Guido was caretaker of this wonderful place that was named after a small lump of land just off the beach a few hundred yards.

Jonny was one of the few kids in the area allowed to swim in the pond and play in the woods and fields. Maybe it was because Uncle Billy was a frequent hired hand, or maybe because Guido thought it better to befriend Jonny than to antagonize him into pranks and such.

He needn't have bothered, Jonny was deathly afraid of him. Guido's eyes, the tone of his voice, the way he said, "Hey you, c'mere," was enough to stop a kid cold, even if he wasn't doing anything. Jonny was so petrified of Guido that once, when the caretaker sent him up a tree to cut down a nuisance limb, Jonny sawed the branch right out from under his feet. Luckily, he landed on his head.

Despite his fears, Jonny loved to play in the fields downwind of the herb gardens. It could have been why he became a chef. All the spices Jonny now uses for his lamb rub used to be grown at Ram Island Farm. This rub is used sparingly so as to blend with, rather than overpower, the lamb.

This recipe makes a quarter-pound of rub and stores fine in the pantry, so it's ready when you are.

- 1 ounce cumin
- 1⅛ ounce granulated garlic
- 1/2 ounce salt
- 1/4 ounce ground coriander
- 1/4 ounce ground oregano
- 1/4 ounce black pepper
- 1/4 ounce dry mustard
- 1/8 ounce ground anise
- 1/8 ounce ground caraway seed
- 1/8 ounce ground rosemary leaves

*Slathering Uncle Billy's
Own Barbeque Sauce
on a bastid rib.*

DESSERTS

Grilled Strawberry Skewers

•

F.B.I. Interstate Indian Pudding

•

Rogue's Bluff Blueberry Ice Cream

•

Death by Chocolate Souffle

Desserts are better served than introduced, so we'll be brief. It's safe to say that Grandmother Alice's pie safe got a lot of use. What with raising Billy, whose sweet tooth is rivaled only by his appetite for barbeque and his thirst for adventure, and later having Jonny always visiting, she kept the key in her apron pocket. Jonny has a bit of a sweet-tooth himself, you understand. A cup of coffee and a brownie hot from the oven is breakfast.

It's no wonder that Jonny's first achievement of culinary note was his dessert-sauce concoction called Death by Chocolate Sauce. So well known, it has become his calling card of sorts.

The four desserts on the pages that follow are particularly well-suited to barbeque; one of them is even cooked on the grill. No matter what the main course, the desserts go fine with them all. As Uncle Billy says, "The barbeque ain't over 'til I've had my puddin'."

Grilled Strawberry Skewers

Come berry season, Jonny and the kids head out to Maxwell Farm behind his mother's house in Cape Elizabeth and fill quart after quart container with native Maine strawberries. Jonny takes the boys because it makes for a good outing. The boys claim he takes them because they're closer to the ground and strawberry picking bothers Jonny's back less when they help. No matter, the result of their efforts is a fun day together topped by a delicious treat at day's end.

- as many strawberries as you like
- enough skewers to hold them
- white sugar
- brown sugar
- sour cream

Clean the strawberries and remove the green tops. Jonny likes to use bamboo skewers, available in kitchen stores and Oriental markets. He soaks the skewers in cold water for a couple of hours before putting four or five berries on each skewer.

Combine equal amounts of brown and white sugar, sift, then roll the skewered strawberries in it. Set the strawberry-laden skewers on a very hot grill for 45 seconds and flip them onto their other side for another 45 seconds. Remove and serve with a dollop of sour cream, or ice cream topped with Jonny's Death By Chocolate sauce.

F.B.I. Interstate Indian Pudding

Just about everyone who has visited Maine, has stopped in Freeport where Mr. L.L. Bean built his now world-famous outdoor supply and clothing business; which means just about everyone who has visited Maine has passed the F.B.I. (Freeport's Big Indian) just off I-95, one exit before Bean's.

The colorfully painted Indian stands about 60-feet tall. When Jonny was a kid, the store behind the Indian sold Indian artifacts and trinkets and such. He remembers being so fascinated with the statue that he used to ask his mother to take him there so just he could play under the tall Indian's shadow. And when Grandmother Alice served Indian Pudding after a meal, he'd save the last bite as an offering to the spirit of Freeport's Big Indian.

- 1 pint whole milk, scalded
- 1 whole vanilla bean
- 1 pound leftover cornbread
- 3 eggs
- 2 cups white sugar
- 2 14-ounce cans evaporated milk
- 1 cup Barbados molasses
- 3 Tablespoons cinnamon
- 3 Tablespoons ground ginger
- 2 ounces black walnut liquor, or rum
- 1/4 stick unsalted butter

Scald the milk in a pan with the vanilla bean, then remove the bean and reserve the scalded milk in a stainless steel bowl.

Put the cornbread in a food processor and, pulse-chop until it's crumb-like. If you don't have a food processor, just whomp it up real good. Put in a mixing bowl and set aside. Beat the eggs, then add, along with the remaining ingredients (except the butter) to the cornbread. Mix thoroughly, using a large wooden spoon.

Grease the inside of a large baking dish with the butter and pour in the pudding. Place the baking dish inside a larger dish and fill the larger dish with water until the water level reaches halfway up the side of the smaller dish. This set-up is called a bain-marie.

Place the pudding (in the bain-marie) in a pre-heated 350°F oven and bake 45 minutes. The pudding is ready when a skewer inserted into the pudding comes out clean.

Spoon the pudding onto plates and serve with whipped cream or ice cream, or both.

Rogue's Bluff Blueberry Ice Cream

Downeast, up to Washington County, where the soil is too shallow to support trees, blueberries grow wild. Every untreed, undeveloped acre is a blueberry field.

By mid-summer everyone's harvesting blueberries. Most kids in Maine earn their first dollars raking blueberries. Migrant workers, retired men and women, anyone with a back to bend and a desire to make a buck can find work in Maine come blueberry season. Farmers usually drive their hay wagons along a route, and like a school bus picking up kids, the farmer picks up his crew early in the morning and drops them off 12 hours later after a day in the fields.

Jonny worked on a crew up north when he was 16. His farmer used a half-sized 1939 International Harvester school bus with a rusted-out floor, two drive gears and brakes that squealed and scraped like they were all drum and no pad. Despite the bus' condition the farmer used to book it along a dirt path of a road hoping to gather his crew and get them into the fields before the sun got hot. The crew was made up of five hard-drinking men all named Beal — Ernie Beal, Eddie Beal, Evan Beal, Ethan Beal and Beal Beal — all from Beal's Island, six Penobscot Indians, four Hare Krishnas from a nearby Ashram, and Jonny.

The day the brakes finally failed, the bus was making time on the downhill approach to Rogue's Bluff. When the farmer braked to round a curve in the road everyone heard the snapping of metal below. The farmer cussed a bit and managed to get the bus around the curve without flipping over or going completely off the road, which was unfortunate because the next curve was sharper and if the bus didn't make that one, they'd be over the bluff for sure.

Ernie Beal, sitting up two rows from Jonny, rolled his head down between his knees, his hands clutched the seat next to him so hard his knuckles were white. The other Beals, probably figuring Ernie had a plan, followed suit. All five Beals dove into their knees, bracing themselves by squeezing the blood out of their hands and the stuffing out of the seats around them. The Hare Krishnas started chanting. In much the manner of the Beals, one started and the others quickly followed. The farmer was still trying to insult the bus into stopping, and the Penobscots simply sat still in their seats. Jonny was scared, but not too scared to decide against doing like the Beals and Hare Krishnas. Having never liked the farmer much, he modeled his behavior after the Indians.

As luck would have it, just where the road widens out before the curve — and the cliff — a moose jumped in front of the bus. The moose got pooched, but not before stopping the bus. After spinning 720 degrees or so, it stopped a good 20 feet from the lip of Rogue's Bluff.

The experience completely changed the farmer, who hosted a feed that night that would have satisfied even Uncle Billy's social nature and dietary needs. The Beals behaved themselves and the Hare Krishnas showed up in full force with tubs of blueberry ice cream churned the day before. They didn't put wine in theirs, but we've added it here to help the ice cream go down.

- 1 pound Maine blueberries
- 4 cups sugar
- 6 eggs, separated
- 2 ounces Maine blueberry wine
- 1½ cups whipping cream
- 6 egg whites
- 1 tray ice cubes

Mash the blueberries with three cups of the sugar. Using a whisk beat together the egg yolks, wine and cream in a stainless steel bowl over almost boiling water, adding the blueberry/sugar mixture as you continue to whisk. When the mixture is frothy, set the bowl in a larger stainless steel bowl containing the ice cubes, and set in the freezer. Whisk the mixture every 30 minutes during the next hour and a half.

Remove the bowl from the freezer and set aside. In another stainless steel bowl, beat the egg whites, adding the remaining sugar and beating until stiff peaks form. Combine the two mixtures in the larger bowl, cover and return to the freezer until ready to serve.

If you like, garnish the ice cream with fresh blueberries and a mint leaf or two, and serve with a chilled glass of blueberry wine.

The young Jonathan St. Laurent and his award-winning Death by Chocolate Layer Cake.

Death By Chocolate Souffle

One measure by which great chefs are judged is their mastery of souffles. Jonny hasn't been called on to do much in the way of souffles since opening Uncle Billy's, but one night such a call did sound, in the unlikely voice of Uncle Billy himself.

In he came that evening, somewhat gussied up, with Carol Anne on his arm. Carol Anne was back in town for her first time since high school, which was when she moved with her family to California. Billy was so upset when she left, he didn't tell the Army physician about his flat feet during his physical the next week; he wanted a change of scenery that bad.

Carol Anne, recently divorced, was "coming home" for some peace of mind. She had looked up Billy from the Jetport phone booth.

Billy had Jonny draw down the lights and jukebox. "Make me a souffle Jonny," he said, "Carol Anne loves souffle."

Jonny stared at the pantry shelves a good 10 minutes trying to figure out how to make a souffle out of barbeque stuff, and then he spied the jars of Death By Chocolate Sauce on the shelf near the cash register.

Jonny's Death By Chocolate Sauce has earned him considerable notoriety, press and praise, but to this day, Uncle Billy's appreciation for that evening's souffle is judgment enough for this chef.

- 9-ounce jar Death By Chocolate Sauce
- 4 egg yolks
- 4 egg whites
- 1/4 cup sugar
- 2 Tablespoons unsweetened cocoa powder
- 1 Tablespoons unsalted butter

Microwave the Death By Chocolate Sauce for 20 seconds, on High. Remove the cap first. Or, submerge the jar halfway into a pot of simmering water for a couple of minutes. Then pour the contents into a stainless steel bowl. Add the egg yolks and stir well with a rubber spatula. In a separate stainless steel bowl, beat the egg whites with the sugar until stiff peaks form, then gently fold in the chocolate mixture from the other bowl.

Melt the butter and, using a small brush, paint the inside of a 1½ quart straight-sided souffle pan. Sprinkle the buttered surface with the cocoa powder. Make sure all surfaces are well coated with butter and cocoa.

Napkin art no. 1124

Pour the souffle mixture into the pan, put into a pre-heated 475°F oven and gently close the oven door. Remove after 15 minutes and serve, preferably with a glass of fine cognac.

Glossary

Abachio: A Roman spit-style whole-animal open-fire method of cooking, usually lamb, goat or pig. Rosemary and garlic aplenty are stuffed into the animal. Also, the name of Jonny's motorized spit.

Acadians: Forebearers of cajuns. Originally from up this way, until unfortunate political events got them shipped off to Louisiana where they had to settle for crawfish instead of that good Gulf of Maine lobster.

Baby Backs: Pork ribs cut from the loin backs of very young pigs. Racks weigh 18 ounces or less. Much favored by the BMW-driving crowd for some unknown reason. See Loin Ribs.

Barbeque: A verb; a noun; a way of life. May be conjugated any way that makes you comfortable, but the result is a uniquely American contribution to the world's great cuisines, the basis of which is live fire and smoke. Not to be confused with grilling and charcoaling.

Bastid Ribs: See Spare Ribs.

Baste: A thin barbeque cooking sauce slathered onto barbeque as it cooks. Bastes vary by region. Jonny employs cider vinegar, molasses and beer in his bastes; a reflection of the Downeast influence in his barbeque.

Bung: A hog casing used to make sausage. Also, to throw something in, as in, "Bung that garlic into the sauce."

Caddy Whoop-Whomp: See Stump Whooped.

Charcoaling: Grilling of steaks and hamburgers and hot dogs directly over a charcoal fire. Also known as grilling, most often occurs in backyards. Not to be confused with "barbequing."

Chopped and pulled: To construct Barbeque Pork Shoulder Sandwiches the meat is pulled, chopped, and then bunged onto the bread.

Cooker: What barbeque is prepared on, or in, as the case may be. May be a $50,000 smokehouse, a Weber grill, or simply a 55-gallon barrel sawed in half. The latter is seen everywhere from Maine agricultural fairs to Jamaican roadside "jerks."

County, The: Aroostook County, Maine's northernmost county, encompassing an area roughly the size of Connecticut. Many towns and villages have no names, and are referred to by letters and numbers. One way or another most of the inhabitants are distantly related to Nephew Jonny by way of his father's side of the family.

Cracklins: Sometimes called *crackles,* these are crisp-fried fatty bits of pork or pork skin, that usually turn up in soul food dishes. Cracklins are also made from the skin of barbequed fish.

Downeast or Down East: All things pertaining to Maine. Named for the prevailing Maine coastal seawinds. Ironically, the further north one sails the further Down East one will end up. Also the geographic origin of American barbeque.

Guma: (pronounced: Goo-ma) The end product of the laborious "boiling down" (reduction) of big kettles of fish, meat and poultry bones, producing a rubber-like essence used to enhance sauces, gyppos and what-have-you. An original Nephew Jonny cooking term.

Gyppo: Originally a derogatory slang term of English derivation for gypsy. Used by Uncle Billy and Jonny to describe gravy, the kind you put on potatoes.

Holy Trinity of Peppers: Black pepper, white pepper and cayenne pepper used in copious quantities in Acadian/cajun cookery.

Jerk Slather: A hot sauce of Caribbean origin. The essential ingredient is the tame-sounding Scotch Bonney (or Bonnet) pepper, also known as a Habanero or Jack-ass pepper. At Uncle Billy's Restaurant the sauce is "slathered" on fish and poultry and then "jerked" around the grill until it's cooked.

Juniper: Heather-like plant cuttings indigenous to Maine that impart a wonderful flavor to live-fire roasted meats, especially game and lamb. Juniper berries have many medicinal uses as well. Uncle Billy will attest to this.

Kippering: Synonymous with barbequing fish. Also called hot smoking, should not be confused with cold smoking, Scottish-smoked salmon for example. Cooking at higher heat and attaining an internal temperature of 85°F distinguishes cold smoking from hot smoking, or kippering.

Loin Ribs: Pork back rib sides weighing no more than two pounds and no less than 18 ounces, or in barbeque-talk, "a two and down rib." Loin ribs are ideal for grilling, though less tender and less meaty than spare ribs.

Mauger: (Pronounced: Mah-gah) A mid-coast Maine term that refers to what some people call "cabin fever" and others call "woods queer." The feeling usually sets in around February and lasts until mud season, which is what Mainers call spring.

Mole: (Pronounced: Mo-lay) A classic Mexican smoked chili and chocolate preparation that predates the Conquistadores. Jonny produces his own, slathers it under the skin of turkeys and barbeques them around Halloween.

Pat Down: See Rub.

Ployes: (Pronounced: Plugs) The staple of French inhabitants of The County (see County, The). Similar to the Russian blini, it is a leavened buckwheat flour pancake often cooked atop a wood-fired cookstove.

Pig-Picking: In days of old, a pig-picking party was a male bonding ritual where an entire wild pig was roasted and consumed on the spit, the meat hand-picked from the carcass piece by roasted piece. Today a pig-picking party is just a fun way to rekindle the hunter/gatherer instinct, and the bonding that takes place is between men and women — which we think is a lot more sensible.

Pinchin': A nocturnal activity undertaken by scurrilous individuals for the express purpose of filling their larders with someone else's agricultural bounty. Said individuals refer to the activity as "moonlighting."

Pit: Technically speaking, pits used to be holes dug in the ground, fires were burned and barbeque prepared in them. Later, the holes in the ground were replaced by mortar and brick structures, but were still called pits. Today, steel and stainless steel cookers like Jonny's are, for some reason, still referred to as pits.

Pit Master: One who cooks traditional barbeque. Sometimes referred to as the High Exalted Master Baster.

Pooched: Having met its demise. As in, "That brisket looks pooched but it sure tastes good."

Porcine: Of or pertaining to swine and all things swinely.

Que: Short for barbeque.

Rack: Pork ribs that are not cut into individual ribs. A six-bone rack has six ribs, a four-bone rack has four. Be wary of the rib joint offering a 14-bone rack. Pigs, no matter where they're from, only have 13.

Ring of Smoke: The pinkish coloration around the inside perimeter of smoked meats. An essential criteria for what Ranger Mel calls, "Respectable barbeque."

Rub: A combination of dry spices, which may or may not include salt, that's rubbed into barbeque meats, fish, poultry and even tofu, before cooking.

Sauce: Divided into two categories: Cooking Sauces and Eating Sauces. The two are not to be confused. The former (also called bastes) is applied to barbeque while it is cooking; the latter is put on the counter in squeeze bottles for you to squirt onto your barbeque. Barbeque joints serve hot and mild varieties.

Shack Fish: A fisherman's private stash, usually traded in pool halls and barrooms for cash, which subsequently buys whiskey, beer and female companionship.

Slab: A whole rack of pork ribs.

Slather: A sauce, baste or just plain ol' margarine applied to meats, fish and poultry before cooking. The act of putting on a slather is slathering. See **Jerk Slather**.

Slurry: A mixture of flour and liquid (usually water) used as a thickening agent in sauces, gravies, stews and pickling mixtures.

Smelting: River ice fishing ritual whereby tidal schools of tiny, bony forage fish are taken on baited hooks by people drinking blackberry brandy and/or schnapps on the pretense of keeping warm.

Spare Ribs: Pork ribs cut from the underside of mature hogs. A rack will generally weigh about three pounds, called a "three and down," by the meat trade. Trimmed of excess bone and cartilage a rack of spare ribs become Jonny's Bastid Ribs. Trimmed once more they are known as St. Louis cut spare ribs. Bastid rib trimmings make for tasty eating either as Trash Ribs, which are cooked and served just like the bastid ribs, or after cooking, he stews them in barbeque sauce for Rib End Sandwiches.

Stump Whooped: Originally a Southern term, having to do with a method of cleaning chitterlins when there is no running water. When Jonny uses the term it refers to the method he employs to kill eels here in Maine, where chitterlins are not a real popular item, but where there is a surplus of tree stumps and eels. **Caddy Whoop-Whomp** is a version of this, employing the fender of a Cadillac instead of a stump. Popular in urban areas. (Ed. Note: It does not need to be your Cadillac, but if it isn't, be prepared to run fast.)

Spit: Sometimes called a rotisserie. A relatively ineffectual method of barbequing large roasts and whole animals. Ineffectual because of the great dissipation of heat that results from cooking over a fire without a cover. Even so, Jonny prefers to cook lamb and mutton in this manner, using mesquite charcoal and juniper vines. See **Abachio.**

Trash Ribs: See Spare Ribs.

Whooped Out: Meat, particularly brisket, cooked until it's ugly on the outside, but tastes some wicked good on the inside. See **Wicked** below.

Wicked: (Pronounced: wick-ette) From the French "c'est terrible," meaning very good, or intense, as in "The jerk sauce was wicked hot."

Where to Find Barbeque Stuff: A Brief Resource Guide

Acadian Smoke Wizards
P.O. Box 2644
South Portland, ME 04106
(207)767-7119
Custom-built barrel cookers, barrel-cooker plans, Tuscan brazier grills, chimney starters, mesquite charcoal, barbeque consultants.

Bland Farms
P.O.Box 506
Glennville, GA 30427-0506
(800)VID-ALIA
Vidalia onions.

The Connecticut Charcoal Co.
1053 Buckley Highway
Union, CT 06076
(203)684-3208
Natural hardwood charcoal, hickory-smoking chips and Light The Bag! (a small bag of natural charcoal coated with canning wax).

L.L. Bean (catalog)
Freeport, ME 04033
(800)221-4221
Cookers, wood chips and tools.

Appledore Smoked Fish
1 Merrill's Wharf
Portland, ME 04112
(207)775-1042
Smoked fish and shellfish, New Zealand venison, mail order ribs and sauces and venison.

Mother's Mountain Mustard
110 Woodville Rd.
Falmouth, ME 04105
(207)781-4658
Mother's Mountain Mustards and other specialty condiments.

Pendery's (catalog)
304 E. Belknap St.
Ft. Worth, TX 76102
(800)533-1870
Spices, mole sauce, Chipotle peppers and more.

Peoples Woods
55 Mill St.
Cumberland, RI 02864
(401)725-2700, or
(508)761-6929
Wood chips and natural charcoals.

Portland Lobster & Bait Co.
48-50 Union Wharf
Portland, ME 04101
(207) 773-1278
Fresh lobster.

'Stache Foods
P.O.Box 705
Damariscotta, ME 04543
(207)529-5879
Uncle Billy's rubs, slathers bastes and sauces. Blackburn's Maple Barbecue Sauce, and other specialty sauces.

Williams-Sonoma (catalog)
P.O. Box 7456
San Francisco, CA 94120-7456
Cookers, wood chips, Vidalia onions and tools.

Willingham World Champion Bar-B-Que
P.O. Box 17312
Memphis, TN 38187-0312
Spices, rubs, sauces and bastes. Commercial barbeque rigs and consultants.

How to Get to
Uncle Billy's SouthSide Barbeque

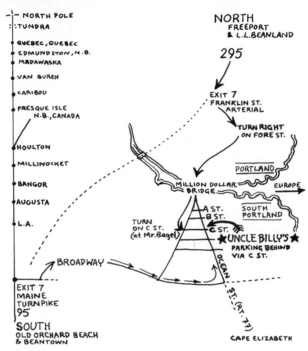

"You can't get there from here," is a familiar saying in Maine that people like to say when they don't know how to direct you to your destination.

But no matter where you are, you can get to Uncle Billy's. We have an airport across town, plenty of slips along the harbor and an Interstate with plenty of ramps for getting on and off.

If you're south, head north; west head east; north head south. The closest land east of Maine, not counting Greenland, is England. You folks will have to fly.

You're all welcome to stop by, slap a quarter in the jukebox and have some fun, Uncle Billy's Downeast Barbeque style.

The End